Taste of Home
SKINNY INSTANT POT®
COOKBOOK

DINNER IN AN INSTANT!

Taste *of* Home
SKINNY INSTANT POT®
COOKBOOK

TASTE OF HOME BOOKS • RDA ENTHUSIAST BRANDS, LLC • MILWAUKEE, WI

© 2020 RDA Enthusiast Brands, LLC.
1610 N. 2nd St., Suite 102, Milwaukee WI 53212-3906

Visit us at *tasteofhome.com* for other *Taste of Home*
books and products.

INTERNATIONAL STANDARD BOOK NUMBER:
978-1-61765-866-2

LIBRARY OF CONGRESS CONTROL NUMBER:
2019945681

EXECUTIVE EDITOR: Mark Hagen
SENIOR ART DIRECTOR: Raeann Thompson
ART DIRECTOR: Maggie Conners
DESIGNER: Jazmin Delgado
COPY EDITOR: Amy Rabideau Silvers
EDITORIAL INTERN: Daniella Peters

COVER:
PHOTOGRAPHER: Dan Roberts
SET STYLIST: Stacey Genaw
FOOD STYLIST: Josh Rink

PICTURED ON FRONT COVER: Mushroom Pot Roast, p. 191
PICTURED ON BACK COVER: Indian-Style Chicken &
Vegetables, p. 148; English Pub Split Pea Soup, p. 231;
Lamb Pitas with Yogurt Sauce, p. 212

Printed in China

1 3 5 7 9 10 8 6 4 2

CONTENTS

GET SOCIAL WITH US!

LIKE US: facebook.com/tasteofhome | **PIN US:** pinterest.com/taste_of_home

FOLLOW US: @tasteofhome | **TWEET US:** twitter.com/tasteofhome

TO FIND A RECIPE:
tasteofhome.com

**TO SUBMIT
A RECIPE:**
tasteofhome.com/
submit

**TO FIND OUT ABOUT
OTHER** *TASTE OF HOME*
PRODUCTS:
shoptasteofhome.com

INSTANT POT® 101

Let's get cooking! It's a snap to simmer a winner any night of the week when you have an Instant Pot and your copy of *Skinny Instant Pot Cookbook* at the ready. These popular devices are a great way for today's cooks to prepare healthy meals. Best of all, each recipe found here was tested in an Instant Pot by the Taste of Home Test Kitchen and reviewed by a registered dietitian, so you're guaranteed success.

WHAT IS AN INSTANT POT?

People may use "instant pot" to refer to any electric pressure cooker, but Instant Pot is actually the brand name for a popular line of electric pressure cookers. The cooker is an airtight pot that cooks food quickly using steam pressure. When it comes to selecting an electric pressure cooker, there are actually several brands and sizes to choose from.

PICK YOUR POT

When determining the best device for you, consider how many people you cook for. This will help narrow the selection to the cooker that's the right size for your needs. Next think about the features various models offer. For example: Is a yogurt-making option something you'd use regularly?

GET TO KNOW THE DESIGN

Electric pressure cookers have a lid that forms an airtight seal to create pressure; an inner pot that holds the food; and an outer pot with a control panel. For the most part, the buttons on the control panel are to help you set a cooking time. For example, if there is a "fish" button, pressing it will likely mean your food will cook for a short time. Some electric pressure cookers have a saute feature and others even offer a sterilize function. Most also include a slow-cook option, which allows you to cook your food slowly instead of pressure-cooking it.

THE PRESSURE'S ON

No matter what cooker you're using, you'll need to learn how to release the pressure safely. Because the escaping steam is hot enough to burn you, it's imperative you read and understand the directions that come with your pot for releasing pressure. Generally speaking, you'll either use a quick-release method (which involves pressing a handle or button) or the natural-release method (where the cooker cools down and releases pressure naturally). Always make sure the hole on top of the pressure-release is facing away from you before pressing the release button. And remember that the quick-release method is not suitable for soups (or anything with a large liquid volume) and cereals (or any dish with a high starch content), because quick-release may cause food to splatter out with the steam.

KEEP IT CLEAN

Follow the manufacturer's directions for cleaning your electric pressure cooker and review the tips and ideas on page 8, and you'll be cooking with it for years to come.

GET THE MOST OUT OF YOUR INSTANT POT®

Today's home cooks are turning to Instant Pots for everything from appetizers to desserts. But are they getting the ultimate out of these incredible kitchen helpers? Review these handy tips and see how you can save even more time and effort when using your Instant Pot.

LEARN HOW TO BOIL WATER (SERIOUSLY)

As soon as you get your cooker, start out by learning how to boil water in it. Pour about 1 cup of water into the inner pot so you will gain a sense of where the maximum fill line is. Seal the lid and select a short cook time. Within 5 minutes, the water should heat up and build pressure, at which point the pressure will release naturally. This is also a good time to learn how to use the quick-release method.

TRY THE RICE COOKER FUNCTION

You can use your pot as a rice cooker. It takes about the same amount of time as cooking on the stovetop, with walk-away convenience, easy cleanup and perfect results every time.

USE IT AS A STEAMER

Looking for a side of steamed veggies? Don't forget that these devices make great steamers. You can even use your Instant Pot to steam hard-boiled eggs—and you won't believe how easy they are to peel.

UP YOUR GAME WITH THE SAUTE FUNCTION

This is one of the reasons people love Instant Pots. The saute function browns meats in the inner pot without dirtying a pan on the stovetop. You can also use this function on the low setting to simmer foods. This means you can simmer stock or beans after pressure-cooking them. And that means you can make super fast soups and stews—all in one pot.

SAVE TIME WITH QUICK-RELEASE

To save time, let the pot cool down slightly, then manually release the pressure. The steam will be very hot, so be careful when moving the release to vent. A cool, wet towel placed on the lid can help speed up the release. Read the release directions that came with your cooker.

The best way to make the most of all-in-one cookers is to first understand what they can do and how they can save you time. A little bit of know-how goes a long way! Turn the page for more tips and hints on using your device.

HOW PRESSURE-COOKING WORKS FOR YOU

Pressure cookers build up hot steam and raise the pressure and temperature to simulate long braising, boiling or simmering. The resulting flavor is just as terrific as if you stood and stirred a bubbling pot all day.

LEARN THE BEST PRACTICES

Using a multipurpose cooker requires some reading and practice, so be patient. It will definitely be worth it in the end. Keep these hints in mind when using your cooker:

- Read the instruction manual for your electric pressure cooker before you make anything. Not all brands and models are the same, so get to know your pot!

- For food safety and efficiency, the total amount of food and liquid should never exceed the maximum level (also known as the max line or the fill line) indicated in the pot.

- Make sure the pressure-release valve is closed before you start cooking. Even the pros at the *Taste of Home* Test Kitchen have forgotten to close the valve and returned to find the pot venting instead of building pressure.

- The pressure-release valve is supposed to feel loose to the touch. The pressure-release handle works simply by applying pressure on the release pipe. Since the contact between the handle and the pipe is not fully sealed, the valve may release a little bit of steam while the food cooks.

- The power cord on some models is removable, which makes the appliance easier to store. If you plug it in and the light does not go on, check the cord. Is it attached securely? When the cooker isn't in use, consider storing the cord in the inner pot.

- After each use, remove and clean the rubber sealing ring, pressure-release valve and anti-block shield. See pages 10 and 11 for more on cleaning your electric pressure cooker.

- If your pot starts to smell like food even after cleaning it, put the sealing ring through the dishwasher. If that doesn't work, try steam cleaning: Pour 2 cups water and 1 Tbsp. lemon zest into the inner pot. Place the lid and run the steam program for 2 minutes. Carefully remove the sealing ring and let it air dry.

- Consider purchasing a separate sealing ring, using one for savory foods and one for sweet treats or foods with delicate flavors.

ARE YOU PLUGGED IN?

STORE CORD IN POT

TO CLEAN, REMOVE RUBBER SEALING RING

SNAP SEAL BACK

FAMILY COOKS SHARE THEIR BEST INSTANT POT® SECRETS

We asked Instant Pot fans to share their favorite hints and tips. Here's how they get the most out of an all-in-one cooker:

THINK BEFORE YOU COOK.
Before you begin cooking, determine if using the Instant Pot is the best method for the job. Not every dish is faster with the Instant Pot; however, the appliance will almost always save you active time. Instead of supervising the entree, you can be playing outside with the kids, relaxing or whipping up a yummy dessert while the main dish simmers.

HIT THE SAUTE FUNCTION EARLY.
Preheating your electric pressure cooker saves valuable time, so turn on the saute function while you prepare the ingredients. Slice and dice your veggies, and your Instant Pot will be ready to saute when you are.

CALCULATE PASTA COOKING TIME.
Check the recommended time for cooking noodles to al dente in boiling water. Halve that time for Instant Pot cooking.

SUBSTITUTE HEALTHY BROWN RICE.
To substitute brown rice for regular white long grain, try increasing the cooking liquid by $\frac{1}{4}$ cup and the cook time by 5 minutes.

ADD THICKENER TO SAUCES.
Because there's no evaporation when you cook with an Instant Pot, braised recipes may have excess liquid. Try bumping up the cornstarch or flour a bit when adapting such recipes to all-in-one cookers.

TRY THESE "HARD-BOILED" EGGS.
Crack a few eggs into a baking dish, then pour a cup of water into your Instant Pot. Set the dish on the trivet insert inside the Instant Pot and pressure-cook on high for 5 minutes. When done, chop up the "egg loaf" for a head start on egg salad.

TURN THE HANDLES INTO LID HOLDERS.
The newer models' lid handles do double duty, holding the Instant Pot open with the lid out of the way. This feature is great for the buffet line. You also can store your Instant Pot this way to ensure the inside fully dries.

LET YOUR INSTANT POT® SHINE

Millions of home cooks have fallen in love with the Instant Pot; maybe you're one of them! If you love something, you need to take care of it. In the case of your all-in-one cooker, that means cleaning and drying it properly each and every time you use it.

Always unplug the device before washing. With the exception of the exterior cooker, or outer pot, all of the Instant Pot's parts are dishwasher safe, making life even easier.

You can allow the parts to dry in the dishwasher, or dry them by hand. Be sure everything, particularly the sealing ring, is completely dry before reassembling and storing.

See the pointers at right for even more washing and cleaning strategies.

WHAT TO WASH AFTER EVERY USE

INNER POT: The inner pot is made of stainless steel, so you can wash it in warm, soapy water or set it in the dishwasher. Since the food touches the pot directly, you'll definitely need to wash this pot after every use.

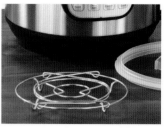

TRIVET INSERT: Since the trivet sits in the inner pot and makes direct contact with the food, you'll need to wash this each time you cook with it. The rack will easily fit in the dishwasher, but feel free to wash by hand and dry completely.

PRESSURE-RELEASE VALVE AND FLOAT VALVE: It's important to wipe food particles off these valves. You don't want anything blocking them, because that would hinder the steam from releasing when you are cooking future meals.

ANTI-BLOCK SHIELD: This is something that many cooks forget to clean. Remove shield from lid. After hand-washing it, wipe with a soft cloth and dry completely. Make sure to secure it in place on the lid before using the appliance again.

SEALING RING: The sealing ring can absorb food odors, so you'll want to clean this after every use. Wash it by hand or toss it in the dishwasher. Make sure it's completely dry before setting it back on the lid. The ring is key to sealing the lid onto the pot and building pressure.

WHAT TO WASH OCCASIONALLY

EXTERIOR: Wipe the exterior of your Instant Pot with a damp cloth as needed. It's important not to submerge the cooker in water since it contains the heating element. When you need to clean the inside of the cooker (not to be confused with the inner pot), use a damp cloth.

LID: After carefully removing the sealing ring and the anti-block shield, wash the lid on the top rack of your dishwasher. It is not necessary to clean the lid after every use, but it's not a bad idea to give it a good wipe with a clean kitchen towel or cotton cloth between washes.

CONDENSATION CUP: This little cup collects the moisture that's created during the cooling process. It doesn't get particularly dirty, so a periodic wash is all it needs. You should check the cup regularly, however, and keep it clean with a quick wipe every now and again.

DEEP-CLEANING BASICS

Show your Instant Pot some extra attention by giving it a deep clean every so often.

INNER POT: To refresh the inner pot, pour 1 cup of white vinegar into it and let sit for 5 minutes. Pour the vinegar out and rinse. If you start to see water stains, use a nonabrasive scouring cleanser to remove them.

SEALING RING: Give the ring a deep clean by adding 2 cups white vinegar and 1 tablespoon lemon zest to the inner pot and running the steam program for 2 minutes. Remove the sealing ring and let it air-dry completely.

SNACKS & APPETIZERS

Got a case of the munchies? Just because you're cutting calories doesn't mean you can't enjoy a savory bite now and then. Perfect for parties and casual nibbles alike, these fast and easy ideas always put hunger in its place.

PARTY PLANNING MADE EASY

Planning is important so you can enjoy your own party. Whether hosting a formal soiree or casual get-together, remember to have fun.

The most important factor to keep in mind when throwing a party is to be sure everyone has a great time—and that includes you! Keep the following ideas in mind for a stress-free bash.

Start by planning healthy appetizers that vary in color, texture and flavor. Serve sweet and spicy, crisp and chewy, hot and cold. Include several make-ahead starters to avoid last-minute prep.

The number of appetizers per person will vary according to the length of the event, the number of guests and the other items on your menu.

For cocktails before dinner, plan on serving 3-4 types of appetizers with enough for 4-5 pieces per person.

For an open house buffet, plan on 4-5 types of appetizers and 4-6 pieces per person.

For a light dinner of finger foods, plan on 6-8 appetizer types and roughly 14-16 pieces per person.

EASY WAY TO IMPRESS

Cheese balls, dips and spreads that contain low-fat cream cheese should stand at room temperature for 15 minutes before serving. They will be easier to spread and far more flavorful.

Dust sweet appetizers with a tiny bit of confectioners' sugar or cocoa powder for a light yet pretty presentation.

Tightly wrap all refrigerated make-ahead appetizers to help them retain optimal texture and flavor.

Keep cold appetizers chilled by setting the serving dish in a bowl of ice. Replenish the ice as it melts.

Prep fresh finger foods to bake and serve in batches.

DO'S AND DONT'S FOR THE PERFECT PARTY

A few simple things can make or break a good time. Run through this list before your guests arrive.

- **Do play music** in the background to set the mood but still allow for easy conversation.

- **Do create an open floor plan** so guests can easily walk from one room to the next. Consider stowing away pieces of furniture that are in the way.

- **Do arrange chairs** in groups that encourage conversation.

- **Don't stash the trash containers** but set them out strategically to prevent clutter from building up.

- **Don't hide the coasters** if you want your guests to use them. Have plenty available and place them in noticeable locations.

- **Don't keep clutter** on tables and other surfaces. Give guests room to easily set down their glasses and plates.

HOW MUCH FOOD? HOW MANY DRINKS?

Planning how much food to serve doesn't have to be daunting!
Here's a quick guide to how many drinks and how much food to stock.

APPETIZERS

Each guest at a dinner party will have about six appetizers (12 if it's a cocktail party). Stock up on bulk items like nuts, pretzels and olives that can fill in any shortfall without drawing attention.

ENTREES AND SIDES

The list below estimates a serving size per person. Remember, the more options you offer, the smaller each portion will be. Given a spread of healthy yet tempting dishes, guests will take a little of each instead of a lot of just one.

- **Poultry, fish or meat:** 6 ounces
- **Grains:** 1.5 ounces as a side dish, 2 ounces as a main dish
- **Potatoes:** 5 ounces
- **Vegetables:** 4 ounces
- **Beans:** 2 ounces
- **Green salad:** 1 ounce
- **Bread:** 1-2 pieces

DRINKS

Several factors govern how many beverages you'll need, including the type of party, its duration and your guests. For a 2-hour party:

- **Ice:** 1 pound per person
- **Nonalcoholic beverages:** One drink per person if alcohol is provided, three per person if alcohol isn't
- **Champagne:** 1.5 glasses per person for cocktails, three glasses per person at dinner
- **Wine:** One bottle of wine for every two adult guests
- **Spirits:** Three drinks per person (you'll get roughly 17 drinks per bottle)

DESSERTS

No matter how big the dinner, there's always room for dessert—especially at the holidays, when everyone looks forward to their favorite cakes or pies. Figure per guest:

- **Cake, tart or pastry:** 1 slice
- **Creamy desserts:** 4 ounces
- **Ice cream:** 5 ounces
- **Cookies:** 5-6 cookies—but because these are the ultimate "just one more" treat, err on the side of plenty. Also take the size of your cookies into account.

CURRIED CHICKEN MEATBALL WRAPS

My strategy to get picky kids to eat healthy: Let everyone assemble their dinner at the table. We love these easy meatball wraps topped with crunchy veggies and peanuts, sweet raisins and a creamy dollop of yogurt.
—Jennifer Beckman, Falls Church, VA

Prep: 35 min.
Cook: 10 min.
Makes: 2 dozen

- 1 large egg,
  lightly beaten
- 1 small onion,
  finely chopped
- ½ cup Rice Krispies
- ¼ cup golden raisins
- ¼ cup minced
  fresh cilantro
- 2 tsp. curry powder
- ½ tsp. salt
- 1 lb. lean ground chicken
- 2 Tbsp. olive oil

SAUCE
- 1 cup plain yogurt
- ¼ cup minced
  fresh cilantro

WRAPS
- 24 small Bibb or Boston
  lettuce leaves
- 1 medium carrot,
  shredded
- ½ cup golden raisins
- ½ cup chopped
  salted peanuts

1. In a large bowl, combine the first 7 ingredients. Add chicken; mix lightly but thoroughly (mixture will be soft). With wet hands, shape mixture into 24 balls (about 1¼-in.). Select saute or browning setting on a 6-qt. electric pressure cooker. Adjust for medium heat; add oil. When oil is hot, brown meatballs in batches; remove and keep warm. Add 1 cup water to pressure cooker. Cook 1 minute, stirring to loosen browned bits from pan. Press cancel.

2. Place trivet insert in pressure cooker. Place meatballs on trivet, overlapping if needed. Lock lid; close pressure-release valve. Adjust to pressure-cook on high for 7 minutes. Quick-release pressure.

3. In a small bowl, mix sauce ingredients. To serve, place 2 tsp. sauce and 1 meatball in each lettuce leaf; top with remaining ingredients. If desired, serve with additional minced fresh cilantro.

1 WRAP: 82 cal., 4g fat (1g sat. fat), 22mg chol., 88mg sod., 6g carb. (4g sugars, 1g fiber), 6g pro. **DIABETIC EXCHANGES:** 1 lean meat, ½ starch.

CILANTRO-LIME CHICKEN WITH SCOOPS

I came up with this recipe when I was preparing for a large party and wanted a healthy Tex-Mex chicken appetizer. The dish can be made ahead of time, and leftovers make for a tasty next-day burrito filling.
—Lori Terry, Chicago, IL

Prep: 15 min.
Cook: 10 min.
Makes: 16 servings

- 1 lb. boneless skinless chicken breasts
- ½ cup reduced-sodium chicken broth
- 2 Tbsp. lime juice
- 2 tsp. chili powder
- 1½ cups frozen petite corn (about 5 oz.), thawed
- 1½ cups chunky salsa
- 1½ cups finely shredded cheddar cheese
- 1 medium sweet red pepper, finely chopped
- 4 green onions, thinly sliced
  Baked tortilla chip scoops
  Minced fresh cilantro

1. Place chicken in a 6-qt. electric pressure cooker; add broth, lime juice and chili powder. Lock lid; close pressure-release valve. Adjust to pressure-cook on high for 7 minutes. Quick-release pressure. A thermometer inserted in chicken should read at least 165°.

2. Remove chicken; discard cooking juices. Shred chicken with 2 forks; return to pressure cooker. Select saute setting and adjust for low heat. Add corn and salsa; cook and stir until heated through, about 5 minutes. Press cancel.

3. Transfer to a large bowl; stir in cheese, red pepper and green onions. Serve with tortilla scoops; sprinkle with cilantro.

¼ **CUP CHICKEN MIXTURE:** 97 cal., 4g fat (2g sat. fat), 26mg chol., 202mg sod., 6g carb. (2g sugars, 1g fiber), 9g pro. **DIABETIC EXCHANGES:** 1 medium-fat meat.

ASIAN WRAPS

This recipe is similar to other Asian wraps but packed with even more deliciously healthy flavor. Instead of ordering Chinese, why not try making these yourself?
—Melissa Hansen, Ellison Bay, WI

Prep: 30 min.
Cook: 10 min.
Makes: 1 dozen

- 2 lbs. boneless skinless chicken breast halves
- ¼ cup reduced-sodium soy sauce
- 6 Tbsp. water, divided
- ¼ cup ketchup
- ¼ cup honey
- 2 Tbsp. minced fresh gingerroot
- 2 Tbsp. sesame oil
- 1 small onion, finely chopped
- 2 Tbsp. cornstarch
- 12 round rice papers (8 in.)
- 3 cups broccoli coleslaw mix
- ¾ cup crispy chow mein noodles

TEST KITCHEN TIP
Rice papers are chewy translucent sheets most often used to hold a combination of savory ingredients. Look for them in the Asian or international aisle.

1. Place chicken in a 6-qt. electric pressure cooker. In a small bowl, whisk soy sauce, ¼ cup water, ketchup, honey, ginger and oil; stir in onion. Pour over the chicken. Lock lid; close pressure-release valve. Adjust to pressure-cook on high for 7 minutes. Quick-release pressure. Press cancel. A thermometer inserted in chicken should read at least 165°. Remove chicken; shred with 2 forks. Set aside.

2. In a small bowl, mix cornstarch and remaining 2 Tbsp. water until smooth; gradually stir into pressure cooker. Select saute setting and adjust for low heat. Simmer, stirring constantly, until thickened, 1-2 minutes. Remove sauce from pressure cooker. Toss shredded chicken with ¾ cup sauce; reserve remaining sauce for serving.

3. Fill a large shallow dish partway with water. Dip a rice paper wrapper into water just until pliable, about 45 seconds (do not soften completely); allow excess water to drip off.

4. Place wrapper on a flat surface. Layer ¼ cup coleslaw, ⅓ cup chicken mixture and 1 Tbsp. noodles across bottom third of wrapper. Fold in both sides of wrapper; fold bottom over filling, then roll up tightly. Place on a serving plate, seam side down. Repeat with remaining ingredients. Serve with reserved sauce.

1 WRAP: 195 cal., 5g fat (1g sat. fat), 42mg chol., 337mg sod., 21g carb. (8g sugars, 1g fiber), 17g pro. **DIABETIC EXCHANGES:** 2 lean meat, 1½ starch, ½ fat.

TROPICAL PULLED PORK SLIDERS

I used what I had in my cupboard to make this Hawaiian-style pork filling, and the results were fantastic. It's a delicious way to fuel a party.
—Shelly Mitchell, Gresham, OR

Prep: 15 min.
Cook: 50 min. + releasing
Makes: 24 servings

- 1 boneless pork shoulder butt roast (3 lbs.), halved
- 2 garlic cloves, minced
- ½ tsp. lemon-pepper seasoning
- 1 can (20 oz.) unsweetened crushed pineapple, undrained
- ½ cup orange juice
- 1 jar (16 oz.) mango salsa
- 24 whole wheat dinner rolls, split

1. Rub roast with garlic and lemon pepper. Transfer to a 6-qt. electric pressure cooker; top with pineapple and orange juice. Lock lid; close pressure-release valve. Adjust to pressure-cook on high for 50 minutes. Let pressure release naturally. A thermometer inserted in pork should read at least 145°.

2. Remove roast; cool slightly. Skim fat from cooking juices. Shred pork with 2 forks. Return pork and cooking juices to pressure cooker. Stir in salsa; heat through. Serve with rolls.

FREEZE OPTION: Freeze cooled meat mixture and juices in freezer containers. To use, partially thaw in refrigerator overnight. Heat through in a saucepan, stirring occasionally and adding a little water if necessary.

1 SLIDER: 211 cal., 7g fat (2g sat. fat), 34mg chol., 349mg sod., 23g carb. (7g sugars, 3g fiber), 13g pro. **DIABETIC EXCHANGES:** 2 medium-fat meat, 1½ starch.

WHY YOU'LL LOVE IT...

"This was very good! I will be adding this to my summer rotation and camping cookbook. Easy to make and delicious, a nice change from traditional pulled pork. Thanks for sharing!"
—PATTY2222, TASTEOFHOME.COM

LIGHT DEVILED EGGS

Our updated version of a classic appetizer uses only half the egg yolks of traditional deviled eggs and calls for soft bread crumbs to help firm up the filling. Light ingredients lower the fat grams even more.
—*Taste of Home* Test Kitchen

Prep: 20 min.
Cook: 5 min. + releasing
Makes: 16 servings

- 8 **large eggs**
- ¼ **cup fat-free mayonnaise**
- ¼ **cup reduced-fat sour cream**
- 2 **Tbsp. soft bread crumbs**
- 1 **Tbsp. prepared mustard**
- ¼ **tsp. salt**
- **Dash white pepper**
- 4 **pimiento-stuffed olives, sliced**
- **Paprika, optional**

1. Place trivet insert and 1 cup water in a 6-qt. electric pressure cooker. Set the eggs on trivet. Lock lid; close pressure-release valve. Adjust to pressure-cook on high for 5 minutes. Let pressure release naturally for 5 minutes; quick-release any remaining pressure. Immediately place eggs in a bowl of ice water to cool. Remove shells.

2. Cut eggs lengthwise in half. Remove yolks; refrigerate 8 yolk halves for another use. Set whites aside. In a small bowl, mash remaining yolks. Stir in mayonnaise, sour cream, bread crumbs, mustard, salt and pepper. Stuff or pipe into egg whites. Garnish with sliced olives. If desired, sprinkle with paprika.

1 STUFFED EGG HALF: 32 cal., 2g fat (1g sat. fat), 46mg chol., 132mg sod., 1g carb. (1g sugars, 0 fiber), 3g pro.

TEST KITCHEN TIP
Amp up flavor without adding fat or calories when you stir your favorite chopped fresh herb into the ingredients for the filling. Try garden-fresh parsley, basil, chives or thyme.

HEALTHY STEAMED DUMPLINGS

My family loves Chinese food, but it's hard to find healthy choices in restaurants or at the grocery store, so I make my own. The recipe makes a lot; I freeze big batches so we can enjoy these dumplings later.
—Melody Crain, Houston, TX

Prep: 45 min.
Cook: 10 min./batch
Makes: 30 dumplings

- ½ cup finely shredded Chinese or napa cabbage
- 2 Tbsp. minced fresh cilantro
- 2 Tbsp. minced chives
- 1 large egg, lightly beaten
- 4 tsp. rice vinegar
- 2 garlic cloves, minced
- 1½ tsp. sesame oil
- ½ tsp. salt
- ½ tsp. ground ginger
- ½ tsp. Chinese five-spice powder
- ¼ tsp. grated lemon zest
- ¼ tsp. pepper
- ¾ lb. lean ground turkey
- 30 pot sticker or gyoza wrappers
- 9 Chinese or napa cabbage leaves
  Sweet chili sauce, optional

1. In a large bowl, combine the first 12 ingredients. Add turkey; mix lightly but thoroughly.

2. Place 1 Tbsp. filling in center of each pot sticker wrapper. (Cover remaining wrappers with a damp paper towel until ready to use.) Moisten wrapper edge with water. Fold the wrapper over filling; seal edges, pleating the front side several times to form a pleated pouch. Stand dumplings on a work surface to flatten bottoms; curve slightly to form crescent shapes, if desired.

3. Place trivet the insert and 1 cup water in a 6-qt. electric pressure cooker. Line trivet with 3 cabbage leaves. Arrange 10 dumplings over cabbage (do not stack). Lock lid; close pressure-release valve. Adjust to pressure-cook on high for 7 minutes; quick-release pressure. A thermometer inserted in dumpling should read at least 165°.

4. Transfer dumplings to a serving plate; keep warm. Discard cabbage and cooking juices. Repeat with additional water, remaining cabbage and dumplings. If desired, serve with the chili sauce.

FREEZE OPTION: Cover and freeze cooled dumplings on parchment-lined baking sheets until firm. Transfer to a large freezer container. To use, microwave dumplings, covered, for 30-45 seconds or until heated through.

1 DUMPLING: 37 cal., 1g fat (0 sat. fat), 14mg chol., 74mg sod., 3g carb. (0 sugars, 0 fiber), 3g pro.

CAPONATA

This Italian eggplant dip preps quickly and actually gets better as it stands. Serve it warm or at room temperature. Try adding a little leftover caponata to scrambled eggs for a savory breakfast the next day.
—Nancy Beckman, Helena, MT

Prep: 20 min.
Cook: 5 min.
Makes: 6 cups

   2 **medium eggplants,
       cut into ½-in. pieces**
   1 **can (14½ oz.) diced
       tomatoes, undrained**
   1 **medium onion,
       chopped**
   ½ **cup dry red wine**
  12 **garlic cloves, sliced**
   3 **Tbsp. extra virgin
       olive oil**
   2 **Tbsp. red wine vinegar**
   4 **tsp. capers, undrained**
   5 **bay leaves**
1½ **tsp. salt**
   ¼ **tsp. coarsely
       ground pepper
       French bread baguette
       slices, toasted
       Optional toppings:
         Fresh basil leaves,
         toasted pine nuts and
         additional olive oil**

1. Place the first 11 ingredients in a 6-qt. electric pressure cooker (do not stir). Lock lid; close pressure-release valve. Adjust to pressure-cook on high for 3 minutes. Quick-release the pressure.

2. Cool slightly; discard bay leaves. Serve with toasted baguette slices. If desired, serve with toppings.

¼ CUP: 34 cal., 2g fat (0 sat. fat), 0 chol., 189mg sod., 5g carb. (2g sugars, 2g fiber), 1g pro.

DID YOU KNOW?
You can make this light bite in your slow cooker. Simply cook the first 11 ingredients on high for 3 hours. Stir together and cook another 2 hours or until the veggies are tender. Discard the bay leaves and serve with the baguettes. Garnish with the toppings, if desired.

BREAKFAST & BRUNCH

Load up on a filling breakfast that keeps your mind off fatty meals the rest of the day. Your Instant Pot® makes it easy. Simply turn the page and learn how delicious it is to brighten up your morning routine.

TAKE MORNINGS TO NEW HEIGHTS

Nothing impresses more than an incredible breakfast or brunch. Whether you're feeding just a few on a busy weekday morning or hosting a crowd for a memorable feast, these eye-opening dishes make every morning a bit more special. Turn here for breakfast favorites made easy as well as tasty new ways to celebrate the day.

EGGS TO THE RESCUE

Few ingredients are as versatile and economical as eggs. That's probably why they're one of the most popular ingredients for your favorite morning fare. Combine eggs with a couple of kitchen staples, and the breakfast possibilities are endless. We have included dozens of egg basics and tips on the following pages to help you make your very best breakfast dishes!

BUYING EGGS

Select eggs with unbroken shells from the refrigerator case. Check the grade: AA, A or B. The higher grades have thicker whites and more nicely shaped yolks.

Read the date on the carton. The USDA requires the carton to display the packing date using the Julian calendar (Jan. 1 is "1" and Dec. 31 is "365"). Other dates on the carton (not required by the USDA) are the sell-by date and the best-by or use-by date. Egg cartons that do not display the USDA shield are governed by individual state standards.

Refrigerate eggs as soon as possible after purchase, discarding any with cracked shells. Always store eggs on an inside shelf in the egg carton. The cartons cushion the eggs and help prevent moisture loss and odor absorption. Do not reuse cartons.

SPECIALTY EGGS

Several types of specialty eggs are commonly available, such as organic, vegetarian, pasteurized, free-range and cage-free. The added cost to produce these eggs is often reflected in their higher price.

Organic Eggs are from hens given feed grown without conventional pesticides, fungicides, herbicides or commercial fertilizers. Organic eggs must meet the standards set by the National Organic Standards Board.

Vegetarian Eggs are from hens fed without animal byproducts.

Pasteurized Eggs are heat-treated to kill salmonella that may be on the shell or in the eggs. Because of the heat treatment, these eggs may have slightly lower levels of heat-sensitive vitamins, such as thiamine and riboflavin.

Free-Range Eggs are from uncaged hens with access to the outdoors.

Cage-Free Eggs are from hens raised indoors without cages.

SHELL COLOR

The color of the eggshell is based on the breed of the chicken and doesn't reflect the contents of the egg itself. Brown and white eggs have identical nutritional values and cook the same.

EGG SIZE EQUIVALENTS

The recipes in this cookbook were tested with large eggs. Use the following guidelines for substituting other egg sizes for large eggs.

EGG SIZE	SUBSTITUTION
1 LARGE EGG	1 JUMBO, 1 EXTRA-LARGE OR 1 MEDIUM
2 LARGE EGGS	2 JUMBO, 2 EXTRA-LARGE, 2 MEDIUM OR 3 SMALL
3 LARGE EGGS	2 JUMBO, 3 EXTRA-LARGE, 3 MEDIUM OR 4 SMALL
4 LARGE EGGS	3 JUMBO, 4 EXTRA-LARGE, 5 MEDIUM OR 5 SMALL

3 WAYS TO CRACK AN EGG

ON THE COUNTER: Gently but firmly rap the egg's equator squarely against the countertop. Use your thumbs to press inward and separate the shell, then pour the yolk and white into a bowl.

WITH TWO EGGS: Hold an egg in each hand. Tap the eggs together at their equators. One egg will crack. Use your thumbs to press inward and separate the shell.

ONE-HANDED: Hold the egg in one hand. Position your thumb and index finger above the egg's equator and your middle and ring fingers below it. Sharply crack the egg against the side of a bowl. Immediately pull the eggshell apart using your thumb and middle finger.

TIPS FOR STORING EGGS

- Refrigerate egg whites in an airtight container up to 4 days.

- Refrigerate unbroken egg yolks covered with water in an airtight container up to 2 days.

- Freeze whole eggs by lightly beating them until blended, then pouring them into an airtight, freezer-safe container. Freeze up to 1 year.

- Freeze egg whites in an airtight container up to 1 year.

- Freeze egg yolks by lightly beating 1/4 cup yolks with 1/8 tsp. salt or 1 1/2 tsp. corn syrup. Pour into a freezer container and store up to 1 year. Use yolks with added salt in savory dishes and yolks with corn syrup for desserts.

FOOD SAFETY WITH EGGS

- Cook eggs until whites and yolks are firm. For dishes that use eggs as an ingredient, such as casseroles, cook until the internal temperature reaches 160°. Discard any egg dishes that have been left at room temperature for more than 2 hours.

CHERRY-ALMOND OATMEAL

Breakfast doesn't get much easier than when you take advantage of your all-in-one cooker and some fruit and nuts for a yummy way to start your day.
—Geraldine Saucier, Albuquerque, NM

Prep: 10 min. + standing
Cook: 5 min. + releasing
Makes: 6 servings

- 4 **cups vanilla almond milk**
- 1 **cup steel-cut oats**
- 1 **cup dried cherries**
- ⅓ **cup packed brown sugar**
- ½ **tsp. salt**
- ½ **tsp. ground cinnamon**

1. In a 6-qt. electric pressure cooker, combine all ingredients. Lock lid; close pressure-release valve. Adjust to pressure-cook on high for 5 minutes. Let pressure release naturally.

2. Let stand 10 minutes before serving (oatmeal will thicken upon standing). If desired, serve with additional almond milk.

¾ **CUP:** 296 cal., 4g fat (0 sat. fat), 0 chol., 304mg sod., 62g carb. (40g sugars, 4g fiber), 4g pro.

TEST KITCHEN TIP
Nutritionally, steel-cut oats are about the same as rolled oats, so take your pick. Skip instant oatmeal mixes, which have a lot of added sugar.

SOUTHWESTERN BREAKFAST CASSEROLE

I created this recipe for a breakfast-for-dinner meal one day, and it's also become a favorite on chilly mornings. Such a wonderful aroma! Extra-sharp cheddar cheese allows you to use less while boosting the flavor.
—Lisa Renshaw, Kansas City, MO

Prep: 20 min. + standing
Cook: 20 min. + releasing
Makes: 4 servings

2 large eggs, room temperature
4 large egg whites, room temperature
⅔ cup fat-free milk
1½ tsp. chili powder
¼ tsp. ground cumin
¼ tsp. cayenne pepper
¼ tsp. pepper
¾ cup canned black beans, rinsed and drained
½ cup frozen corn, thawed
½ cup cubed fully cooked ham
½ cup shredded extra-sharp cheddar cheese
¼ cup canned chopped green chiles
3 slices whole wheat bread, lightly toasted and cubed
Pico de gallo, optional

1. In a large bowl, whisk together the first 7 ingredients. Stir in beans, corn, ham, cheese and chiles. Stir in toasted bread cubes to moisten.

2. Transfer to a greased 1½-qt. baking dish. Place trivet insert and 1 cup water in pressure cooker. Cover baking dish with foil. Fold an 18x12-in. piece of foil lengthwise into thirds to make a sling. Use the sling to lower the dish onto the trivet.

3. Lock lid; close pressure-release valve. Adjust to pressure-cook on high for 20 minutes. Let pressure release naturally for 10 minutes; quick-release any remaining pressure. Using foil sling, carefully remove baking dish. Uncover and let stand 10 minutes before serving. If desired, serve with pico de gallo.

1¼ CUPS: 257 cal., 9g fat (4g sat. fat), 118mg chol., 661mg sod., 23g carb. (4g sugars, 4g fiber), 21g pro. **DIABETIC EXCHANGES:** 3 lean meat, 1½ starch.

RAISIN NUT OATMEAL

There's no better feeling than starting off the day with a nourishing breakfast. I love that the oats, fruit and spices in this homey meal cook together on their own.
—Valerie Sauber, Adelanto, CA

Prep: 10 min. + standing
Cook: 5 min. + releasing
Makes: 6 servings

- 3 cups vanilla almond milk
- ¾ cup steel-cut oats
- ¾ cup raisins
- 3 Tbsp. brown sugar
- 4½ tsp. butter
- ¾ tsp. ground cinnamon
- ½ tsp. salt
- 1 large apple, peeled and chopped
- ¼ cup chopped pecans

1. In a 6-qt. electric pressure cooker, combine first 7 ingredients. Lock lid; close pressure-release valve. Adjust to pressure-cook on high for 5 minutes. Let pressure release naturally.

2. Stir in apple. Let stand 10 minutes before serving (oatmeal will thicken upon standing). Spoon oatmeal into bowls; sprinkle with pecans.

¾ CUP: 272 cal., 9g fat (2g sat. fat), 8mg chol., 298mg sod., 47g carb. (29g sugars, 4g fiber), 4g pro.

WHY YOU'LL LOVE IT...

"I tried this recipe with almond milk and it was fabulous! My entire family loved it! So delicious!"
—HON1HON1, TASTEOFHOME.COM

EGGS IN PURGATORY

Tomatoes and red pepper flakes add spicy zing to these saucy eggs. Serve them with toasted bread or sauteed polenta rounds for an unforgettable morning meal.
—Nick Iverson, Denver, CO

Prep: 30 min.
Cook: 5 min.
Makes: 4 servings

- 2 cans (14½ oz. each) fire-roasted diced tomatoes, undrained
- 1 medium onion, chopped
- ½ cup water
- 2 Tbsp. canola oil
- 2 garlic cloves, minced
- 2 tsp. smoked paprika
- ½ tsp. sugar
- ½ tsp. crushed red pepper flakes
- ¼ cup tomato paste
- 4 large eggs
- ¼ cup shredded Manchego or Monterey Jack cheese
- 2 Tbsp. minced fresh parsley
- 1 tube (18 oz.) polenta, sliced and warmed, optional

1. Place the first 8 ingredients in a 6-qt. electric pressure cooker. Lock lid; close pressure-release valve. Adjust to pressure-cook on high for 4 minutes. Quick-release pressure. Press cancel.

2. Select saute setting and adjust for low heat. Add tomato paste; simmer, uncovered, until mixture is slightly thickened, about 10 minutes, stirring occasionally.

3. With the back of a spoon, make 4 wells in sauce. Break an egg into each well; sprinkle with cheese. Cover (do not lock lid). Simmer until egg whites are completely set and yolks begin to thicken but are not hard, 8-10 minutes. Sprinkle with parsley. If desired, serve with polenta.

1 SERVING: 255 cal., 14g fat (4g sat. fat), 193mg chol., 676mg sod., 20g carb. (9g sugars, 3g fiber), 11g pro. **DIABETIC EXCHANGES:** 1½ fat, 1 starch, 1 medium-fat meat.

APPLE PIE STEEL-CUT OATMEAL

I absolutely love this one-dish oatmeal. The steel-cut oats have so much flavor and texture. My family loves to sprinkle toasted pecans on top.
—Angela Lively, Conroe, TX

Prep: 10 min. + standing
Cook: 5 min. + releasing
Makes: 8 servings

  6 cups water
1½ cups steel-cut oats
1½ cups unsweetened
     applesauce
  ¼ cup maple syrup
1½ tsp. ground cinnamon
  ½ tsp. ground nutmeg
  ⅛ tsp. salt
  1 large apple, chopped
     Optional toppings:
        Sliced apples and
        toasted pecans

1. In a 6-qt. electric pressure cooker, combine the first 7 ingredients. Lock lid; close pressure-release valve. Adjust to pressure-cook on high for 5 minutes. Let the pressure release naturally.

2. Stir in chopped apple. Let stand 10 minutes before serving (oatmeal will thicken upon standing). If desired, top servings with sliced apples, pecans and additional syrup.

1¼ CUPS: 171 cal., 2g fat (0 sat. fat), 0 chol., 39mg sod., 36g carb. (13g sugars, 4g fiber), 4g pro.

TEST KITCHEN TIP
Boost the protein power in this oatmeal with a dollop of vanilla Greek yogurt. Not only will it add layers of flavor and texture, but it will help you stay full longer.

HAWAIIAN BREAKFAST HASH

Breakfast is our favorite meal, and we love a wide variety of dishes. This hash brown recipe is full of flavor and possibilities. Top it with some eggs or spinach for another twist!
—Courtney Stultz, Weir, KS

Prep: 30 min.
Cook: 5 min.
Makes: 6 servings

- 4 bacon strips, chopped
- 1 Tbsp. canola or coconut oil
- 2 large sweet potatoes (about 1½ lbs.), peeled and cut into ½-in. pieces
- 1 cup water
- 2 cups cubed fresh pineapple (½-in. cubes)
- ½ tsp. salt
- ¼ tsp. chili powder
- ¼ tsp. paprika
- ¼ tsp. pepper
- ⅛ tsp. ground cinnamon

1. Select the saute or browning setting on a 6-qt. electric pressure cooker; adjust for medium heat. Add bacon; cook and stir until crisp. Remove with a slotted spoon; drain on paper towels. Discard drippings.

2. Add oil to pressure cooker. When oil is hot, brown sweet potato pieces in batches. Remove from pressure cooker. Add water to pressure cooker. Cook 1 minute, stirring to loosen browned bits from pan. Press cancel. Place steamer basket in pressure cooker.

3. Stir pineapple and seasonings into potatoes; transfer to steamer basket. Lock lid; close pressure-release valve. Adjust to pressure cook on high for 2 minutes. Quick-release pressure. Sprinkle with the bacon.

⅔ **CUP:** 194 cal., 5g fat (1g sat. fat), 6mg chol., 309mg sod., 35g carb. (17g sugars, 4g fiber), 4g pro. **DIABETIC EXCHANGES:** 2 starch, 1 fat.

GRUYERE & PROSCIUTTO STRATA

Prosciutto, sweet onions and Gruyere combine for a perfect brunch dish that's extra flavorful for a lighter dish, and the recipe's just the right size for us.
—Patti Lavell, Islamorada, FL

Prep: 15 min. + standing
Cook: 20 min. + releasing
Makes: 5 servings

- 1 tsp. canola oil
- 2 oz. thin slices prosciutto, chopped
- 1 large sweet onion, chopped (2 cups)
- ½ cup egg substitute
- 1¼ cups 2% milk
- ⅛ tsp. ground mustard
  Dash pepper
- 4 cups cubed French bread
- ¾ cup shredded Gruyere or Swiss cheese, divided

1. Select saute setting on a 6-qt. electric pressure cooker and adjust for medium heat; add oil. When oil is hot, cook and stir prosciutto until crisp, about 3 minutes. Remove from pan with a slotted spoon. Add onion to pressure cooker; cook and stir until tender, 4-5 minutes. Press cancel.

2. In a large bowl, whisk egg substitute, milk, mustard and pepper. Stir in bread, half the cheese, and onions. Reserve 2 Tbsp. cooked prosciutto for topping; stir the remaining prosciutto into bread mixture.

3. Transfer to a greased 1½-qt. baking dish. Wipe pressure cooker clean. Place trivet insert and 1 cup water in pressure cooker. Cover baking dish with foil. Fold an 18x12-in. piece of foil lengthwise into thirds, making a sling. Use the sling to lower the dish onto the trivet.

4. Lock lid; close pressure-release valve. Adjust to pressure-cook on high for 20 minutes. Let pressure release naturally for 10 minutes; quick-release any remaining pressure. Using foil sling, carefully remove baking dish. Sprinkle with remaining cheese and prosciutto; cover and let stand 10 minutes.

1 CUP: 241 cal., 10g fat (5g sat. fat), 34mg chol., 557mg sod., 22g carb. (8g sugars, 1g fiber), 16g pro. **DIABETIC EXCHANGES:** 2 medium-fat meat, 1½ starch, 1 fat.

HOMEMADE CHUNKY APPLESAUCE

This applesauce is so easy. My family loves the things I make from scratch, and it's good knowing exactly what I'm putting in it!
—Marilee Cardinal, Burlington, NJ

Prep: 10 min.
Cook: 5 min. + releasing
Makes: 5 cups

  7 **medium McIntosh, Empire or other apples (about 3 lbs.)**
 ½ **cup sugar**
 ½ **cup water**
  1 **Tbsp. lemon juice**
 ¼ **tsp. almond or vanilla extract**

1. Peel, core and cut each apple into 8 wedges. Cut each wedge crosswise in half; place in a 6-qt. electric pressure cooker. Add remaining ingredients.

2. Lock lid; close pressure-release valve. Adjust to pressure-cook on high for 3 minutes. Let pressure release naturally. Mash apples with a potato masher or use an immersion blender until desired consistency is reached.

¾ **CUP:** 139 cal., 0 fat (0 sat. fat), 0 chol., 0 sod., 36g carb. (33g sugars, 2g fiber), 0 pro.

WHY YOU'LL LOVE IT...

"Super easy, loved the flavor. I added just a touch of cinnamon also."

—HOTFUDGESUNDAE, TASTEOFHOME.COM

CINNAMON BLUEBERRY FRENCH TOAST

Healthy and hearty! That's the best way to describe this satisfying breakfast. It's one dish worth jumping out of bed for.
—Angela Lively, Conroe, TX

Prep: 15 min. + standing
Cook: 20 min. + releasing
Makes: 4 servings

2 large eggs
1⅓ cups 2% milk
3 Tbsp. sugar
1 tsp. ground cinnamon
1 tsp. vanilla extract
¼ tsp. salt
6 cups cubed French bread (about 6 oz.)
¾ cup fresh or frozen blueberries
Maple syrup

HEALTH TIP
Swap whole wheat for white French bread to increase the fiber in this recipe. If you can't find it, cube 100% whole wheat buns.

1. Whisk together the first 6 ingredients. Arrange half the bread cubes in a greased 1½-qt. baking dish. Top with half the blueberries and half the milk mixture. Repeat layers.

2. Place trivet insert and 1 cup water in a 6-qt. electric pressure cooker. Cover baking dish with foil. Fold an 18x12-in. piece of foil lengthwise into thirds, making a sling. Use the sling to lower the dish onto the trivet.

3. Lock lid; close pressure-release valve. Adjust to pressure-cook on high for 20 minutes. Let pressure release naturally for 10 minutes; quick-release any remaining pressure. Using foil sling, carefully remove baking dish. Let stand 10 minutes. Serve with syrup.

1 SERVING: 273 cal., 6g fat (2g sat. fat), 100mg chol., 479mg sod., 44g carb. (19g sugars, 2g fiber), 11g pro.

RHUBARB COMPOTE WITH YOGURT

My grandma made rhubarb compote and always had some in the freezer when I came to visit. This breakfast is a tribute to her. No two batches of rhubarb are exactly alike, so make sure to taste your compote before you chill it. It should be tart, but sometimes it needs a little extra sugar.

—Michael Hoffman, Brooklyn, NY

Prep: 10 min. + chilling
Cook: 5 min. + releasing
Makes: 6 servings

- 2 **cups finely chopped fresh rhubarb**
- ⅓ **cup water**
- ¼ **cup sugar**
- 3 **cups reduced-fat plain Greek yogurt**
- 2 **Tbsp. honey**
- ¾ **cup sliced almonds, toasted**

1. Place rhubarb, water and sugar in a 6-qt. electric pressure cooker. Lock lid; close pressure-release valve. Adjust to pressure-cook on high 3 minutes. Let pressure release naturally for 10 minutes, then quick-release any remaining pressure. Transfer to a bowl; cool slightly. Refrigerate until cold.

2. In a small bowl, whisk yogurt and honey until blended. Spoon into serving dishes. Top with compote; sprinkle with the almonds.

½ CUP YOGURT WITH ABOUT 2 TBSP. COMPOTE AND 2 TBSP. ALMONDS: 216 cal., 8g fat (2g sat. fat), 7mg chol., 49mg sod., 23g carb. (20g sugars, 2g fiber), 14g pro. **DIABETIC EXCHANGES:** 1 starch, 1 reduced-fat milk, 1 fat.

SIDE DISHES

When it's time to round out a healthy meal, let your one-pot cooker do the work. From classic sides to ethnic favorites, these trimmed-down dishes make any menu a bit more special.

FARM-FRESH PICKIN'S
Here's what's best to buy according to the season.

SPRING
Artichokes, Arugula, Asparagus, Avocados, Butter Lettuce, Chard, Green Beans, Mango, Morel Mushrooms, Parsnips, Radishes, Rhubarb, Snap Peas, Spinach, Strawberries

SUMMER
Apricots, Baby Carrots, Cherries, Cucumbers, Bell Peppers, Blueberries, Boysenberries, Cantaloupe, Corn, Eggplant, Figs, Green Beans, Key Limes, Lima Beans, Long Beans, Melon, Okra, Onions, Peaches, Pineapple, Raspberries, Snap Peas, Snow Pea , Tomatoes, Watermelon, Zucchini

FALL

Acorn Squash, Apples, Beets, Broccoli, Cauliflower, Celery, Cranberries, Endive, Garlic, Ginger, Grapes, Jalapeno Peppers, Kohlrabi, Mushrooms, Pears, Potatoes, Pumpkin, Quince, Sweet Potatoes

WINTER
Brussels Sprouts, Cabbage, Dates, Grapefruit, Horseradish, Kale, Mandarin Oranges, Passion Fruit, Radicchio, Tangerines, Turnips, Winter Squash

WHAT'S DOES YOUR PRODUCE LABEL MEAN?

GMO AND NON-GMO
GMO stands for genetically modified organism. Produce labeled GMO has been engineered via DNA modification to be larger or more abundant, or to withstand drought or insect damage. Produce labeled non-GMO has not been modified in this way.

NATURAL
In theory, foods with this label are produced simply, without food additives, antibiotics, added colors or artificial sweeteners. That said, the Food and Drug Administration has no official regulations about manufacturers' use of the "natural" label.

USDA ORGANIC
This label signifies crops grown without the use of pesticides or chemicals and without genetic modification. If you see this logo on packaging, it's got the official stamp of approval from the U.S. Department of Agriculture.

WHY ORGANICS COST MORE
- Organic foods take longer to grow, with no chemicals or hormones to speed things up.
- Organic farms are typically smaller than traditional ones.
- Organic farming is usually more labor-intensive.

GUIDE TO RICE & GRAINS

Rice is used in many cuisines around the globe. In fact, there are more than 40,000 known types of rice in the world. As North American interest in world cuisines has increased, the selection and availability of rice varieties has expanded on our supermarket shelves.

WHITE & BROWN RICE

The most common types of rice used in American cooking are white and brown. White rice can be stored indefinitely in an airtight container. Brown rice should be stored at room temperature for no more than 6 months. For longer storage, refrigerate or freeze.

ARBORIO RICE

This is a medium-grain rice used for making risotto. When cooked into creamy textured risotto, it has a chewy center.

AROMATIC RICE

Also know as fragrant rice, aromatic rice has an incredible perfume while cooking and a very distinctive flavor. Each type—basmati, Black Japonica, jasmine and Texmati—has its own cooking characteristics, which can change from one growing season to the next.

WILD RICE

This is not actually rice; it's a marsh grass grain. Wild rice can be stored indefinitely in an airtight container. Rinse wild rice before cooking to remove any dirt or debris. Note that wild rice may not absorb all of the cooking liquid before it becomes tender. Drain off any liquid that remains in the pot.

COOKING RICE & GRAINS

The chart at right tells you more about a variety of grains and their uses. You might want to cook them or rice on the stovetop while using your one-pot cooker for an entree. Bring water, ¼ tsp. salt (if desired) and 1 Tbsp. butter (if desired) to a boil in a 2-qt. saucepan. Stir in the rice or grain; return to a boil. Cover and reduce heat to a simmer. Cook for the time given on the package or until tender. Fluff with a fork and serve.

BROWN RICE: EASY AS 1, 2, 3

The standard ratio for long grain rice (white or brown) is 1-2-3:
1 cup uncooked rice
+ 2 cups liquid
= 3 cups cooked rice.

Brown rice takes 40-50 minutes to cook but has about four times the fiber of white rice. Quick and instant brown rice cook in about 10 minutes and are just as healthy, so take a shortcut!

GRAIN	DESCRIPTION	STORAGE
BARLEY	A flavorful, chewy alternative to white rice, pearl, quick-cooking and Scotch barley can be found in supermarkets. Pearl barley has the double outer hull and bran layer removed. Quick-cooking barley is precooked pearl barley. Scotch barley has been processed less than pearl barley and retains some of its bran layer.	Store barley in an airtight container in a cool, dry place. Barley can also be stored in the refrigerator or freezer.
BUCKWHEAT	Buckwheat is not related to wheat, which means it is gluten-free. The black triangular seeds are sold as groats, buckwheat grits, kasha or buckwheat flour. Groats are kernels with the inedible black shells removed. Grits are finely ground unroasted groats. Kasha is roasted groats that have been cracked into coarse, medium or fine grains. Buckwheat flour, used for noodles, pancakes and breads, is made of ground groats.	Store opened buckwheat products in a cool, dry place (in warm climates, use the refrigerator or freezer). Always store buckwheat flour in the refrigerator.
BULGUR	This whole wheat grain is processed like converted rice. Kernels are cleaned, steam-cooked, dried and cracked or ground into pieces. Bulgur is ready to eat after soaking in water or broth for about 30 minutes. Bulgur comes in coarse, medium and fine grains. Coarse bulgur is used for stuffings and pilafs; medium for cereals, breads and stews; and fine for tabbouleh, cereals and breads.	Store opened packages of bulgur in a cool, dry place for up to 1 month. In warm climates, store it in the refrigerator or freezer.
CORNMEAL	Dried corn is hulled and finely ground between steel rollers or two stones to make meal. Stone-ground cornmeal is coarser than steel-ground and has a shorter shelf life. Look for white and yellow cornmeal in supermarkets and for blue cornmeal in specialty markets. Self-rising cornmeal has added baking powder and salt and cannot be used interchangeably with plain cornmeal. Use cornmeal for breads, muffins and polenta.	Store stone-ground cornmeal in the refrigerator for up to 4 months. Use steel-ground cornmeal before the use-by date on the package.
GRITS	Grits is a term used to describe coarsely ground dried corn, oats or rice. Today, it typically refers to coarsely ground dried hominy (field corn). Hominy grits are sold as regular grits, quick-cooking grits and, with the shortest cooking time, instant grits.	Use before the use-by date on the package.
MILLET	This grain makes a healthy side dish. Look for it in health-food stores and some grocery stores. Pearl millet comes in white, yellow, red or gray. To cook as a substitute for rice, simmer ½ cup millet in 1½ cups water in a covered saucepan for about 25 minutes until fluffy.	Store millet in an airtight container in a cool, dry place for several months.
HOMINY	Dried corn with the hull and germ removed through a process of soaking in an alkaline solution, typically lye or slacked lime, is called hominy. It's available canned or dried. When ground, it is often referred to as grits.	Use before the use-by date on the package.
OATS	Popular and readily available, oats are a grain and breakfast cereal. The most common oat products are Scottish or steel-cut, old-fashioned, quick-cooking and instant. Scottish oats have been processed less than the old-fashioned oats. Old-fashioned oats have been flattened by rollers; quick-cooking oats are flattened and cut into small pieces; instant oats have been precooked, dried, and cut even smaller. Oat bran is the outer bran layer of the grain and is high in fiber. Old-fashioned and quick-cooking oats can be used interchangeably in baked goods. Instant oats cannot be used interchangeably with other oat products.	Once opened, oats should be stored in a cool, dry place. In warm climates, store them in the freezer or refrigerator. Use by the package use-by date.
QUINOA	Quinoa has a more complete protein than most grains. The flattened oval grains come in a variety of colors, most commonly white, pale gold, black and red. Look for quinoa in the grains, rice or organic food aisles of grocery stores. Rinse under cold running water before cooking. For a more pronounced flavor, toast in a skillet before cooking. Quinoa is done when the grains are translucent and the germ spirals out to form a crunchy tail. Quinoa has a mild taste and a fluffy texture.	Store uncooked quinoa in a cool, dry place. In warm climates, store it in the refrigerator or freezer.

SUMMER SQUASH

We love squash, but I got tired of fixing plain old squash and cheese. I decided to jazz it up a bit. This was a huge hit with the family.
—Joan Hallford, North Richland Hills, TX

Prep: 20 min.
Cook: 5 min.
Makes: 8 servings

- 1 lb. medium yellow summer squash
- 1 lb. medium zucchini
- 2 medium tomatoes, chopped
- 1 cup vegetable broth
- ¼ cup thinly sliced green onions
- ½ tsp. salt
- ¼ tsp. pepper
- 1½ cups Caesar salad croutons, coarsely crushed
- ½ cup shredded cheddar cheese
- 4 bacon strips, cooked and crumbled

1. Cut squash into ¼-in. -thick slices; place in a 6-qt. electric pressure cooker. Add tomatoes, broth, green onions, salt and pepper. Lock lid; close pressure-release valve. Adjust to pressure-cook on high for 1 minute. Quick-release pressure. Remove squash with a slotted spoon.

2. To serve, top with croutons, cheese and bacon.

¾ **CUP:** 111 cal., 6g fat (2g sat. fat), 12mg chol., 442mg sod., 10g carb. (4g sugars, 2g fiber), 6g pro. **DIABETIC EXCHANGES:** 1 vegetable, 1 fat.

SICILIAN STEAMED LEEKS

I love the challenge of developing recipes for my garden leeks, a delicious but underused vegetable. This Italian-flavored dish is an all-time favorite.
—Roxanne Chan, Albany, CA

Prep: 10 min.
Cook: 5 min.
Makes: 6 servings

1 large tomato, chopped
1 small navel orange, peeled, sectioned and chopped
2 Tbsp. minced fresh parsley
2 Tbsp. sliced Greek olives
1 tsp. capers, drained
1 tsp. red wine vinegar
1 tsp. olive oil
½ tsp. grated orange zest
½ tsp. pepper
6 medium leeks (white portion only), halved lengthwise, cleaned
Crumbled feta cheese

1. Combine the first 9 ingredients; set aside. Place trivet insert and 1 cup water in a 6-qt. electric pressure cooker. Set leeks on trivet. Lock lid; close pressure-release valve. Adjust to pressure-cook on high for 2 minutes. Quick-release pressure.

2. Transfer leeks to a serving platter. Spoon tomato mixture over top; sprinkle with cheese.

1 SERVING: 83 cal., 2g fat (0 sat. fat), 0 chol., 77mg sod., 16g carb. (6g sugars, 3g fiber), 2g pro. **DIABETIC EXCHANGES:** 1 starch, ½ fat.

TEST KITCHEN TIP
To prepare leeks, remove any withered outer leaves. Trim root end. Cut off and discard the green upper leaves at the point where the pale green becomes dark green. Leeks often contain sand between their many layers. If leeks are to be sliced or chopped, cut the leek open lengthwise down one side and rinse under cold running water, separating the leaves.

SPAGHETTI SQUASH WITH TOMATOES

This squash is tempting as a side dish, but you can also top it with canned tuna to serve as an entree. I use my own home-canned tomatoes for the best flavor. It's easy, tasty and light!
—Carol Chase, Sioux City, IA

Prep: 15 min.
Cook: 10 min.
Makes: 10 servings

- 1 medium spaghetti squash, halved lengthwise, seeds removed
- 1 can (14 oz.) diced tomatoes, drained
- ¼ cup sliced green olives with pimientos
- 1 tsp. dried oregano
- ½ tsp. salt
- ½ tsp. pepper
- ½ cup shredded cheddar cheese
- ¼ cup minced fresh basil

1. Place trivet insert and 1 cup water in a 6-qt. electric pressure cooker. Set the squash on trivet, overlapping as needed to fit. Lock lid; close pressure-release valve. Adjust to pressure-cook on high for 7 minutes. Quick-release pressure. Press cancel.

2. Remove squash and trivet from pressure cooker; drain cooking liquid from pressure cooker. Using a fork, separate squash into strands resembling spaghetti, discarding skin. Return squash to pressure cooker. Stir in tomatoes, olives, oregano, salt and pepper. Select saute setting and adjust for low heat. Cook and stir until heated through, about 3 minutes. Top with cheese and basil.

¾ **CUP:** 92 cal., 3g fat (1g sat. fat), 6mg chol., 296mg sod., 15g carb. (1g sugars, 4g fiber), 3g pro. **DIABETIC EXCHANGES:** 1 starch, ½ fat.

PRESSURE-COOKER DRESSING

Here's an easy dressing that's perfect for special get-togethers. It's a modern take on an old-fashioned side dish that everyone loves.
—Rita Nodland, Bismarck, ND

Prep: 15 min. + standing
Cook: 10 min. + releasing
Makes: 8 servings

 2 **Tbsp. olive oil**
 1 **medium celery**
   rib, chopped
 1 **small onion, chopped**
 2 **cups reduced-sodium**
   chicken broth
 1 **tsp. poultry seasoning**
 ¼ **tsp. salt**
 ¼ **tsp. pepper**
 8 **cups unseasoned**
   stuffing cubes

1. Select saute setting on a 6-qt. electric pressure cooker. Adjust for medium heat; add oil. When oil is hot, cook and stir celery and onion until crisp-tender, 3-4 minutes. Press cancel. Stir in broth and seasonings. Gently stir in stuffing cubes; toss to combine. Transfer to a greased 1½-qt. baking dish.

2. Place trivet insert and 1 cup water in pressure cooker. Cover baking dish with foil. Fold an 18x12-in. piece of foil lengthwise into thirds, making a sling. Use the sling to lower the dish onto the trivet.

3. Lock lid; close pressure-release valve. Adjust to pressure-cook on high for 15 minutes. Let pressure release naturally for 10 minutes; quick-release any remaining pressure. Using foil sling, carefully remove baking dish. Let stand 10 minutes.

½ **CUP:** 225 cal., 5g fat (0 sat. fat), 0 chol., 634mg sod., 40g carb. (3g sugars, 3g fiber), 8g pro.

BUFFALO WING POTATOES

I was getting tired of mashed potatoes and baked spuds, so I decided to create something new. This potluck-ready recipe is an easy and delicious twist on the usual potato dish.
—Summer Feaker, Ankeny, IA

Prep: 15 min.
Cook: 5 min.
Makes: 6 servings

2 lbs. Yukon Gold potatoes, cut into 1-in. cubes
1 small sweet yellow pepper, chopped
½ small red onion, chopped
¼ cup Buffalo wing sauce
½ cup shredded cheddar cheese
Optional toppings: Crumbled cooked bacon, sliced green onions and sour cream

1. Place steamer basket and 1 cup water in a 6-qt. electric pressure cooker. Set potatoes, yellow pepper and onion in basket. Lock lid; close pressure-release valve. Adjust to pressure-cook on high for 3 minutes. Quick-release pressure. Press cancel.

2. Remove vegetables to a serving bowl; discard cooking liquid. Add Buffalo wing sauce to vegetables; gently stir to coat. Sprinkle with cheese. Cover and let stand until cheese is melted, 1-2 minutes. If desired, top with bacon, green onions and sour cream.

¾ **CUP:** 182 cal., 4g fat (2g sat. fat), 9mg chol., 382mg sod., 32g carb. (3g sugars, 3g fiber), 6g pro. **DIABETIC EXCHANGES:** 2 starch, ½ fat.

WHY YOU'LL LOVE IT...

"Such a delicious recipe! Don't skip the green onions or bacon! Would be great for a picnic or potluck."
—LPH, TASTEOFHOME.COM

MUSHROOM RICE PILAF

A few modifications to our Great-Aunt Bernice's easy pilaf recipe made it a much-requested item for potlucks, barbecues and family get-togethers. It'll become a favorite in your home and with your gang, too!
—Amy Williams, Rialto, CA

Prep: 20 min.
Cook: 5 min. + releasing
Makes: 6 servings

¼ **cup butter**
1 **cup medium grain rice**
½ **lb. sliced baby portobello mushrooms**
6 **green onions, chopped**
2 **garlic cloves, minced**
1 **cup water**
4 **tsp. beef base**

1. Select saute setting on a 6-qt. electric pressure cooker. Adjust for medium heat; add butter. When butter is hot, cook and stir rice until lightly browned, 3-5 minutes. Press cancel. Add mushrooms, green onions and garlic. In a small bowl, whisk water and beef base; pour over rice mixture.

2. Lock lid; close pressure-release valve. Adjust to pressure-cook on high for 4 minutes. Let pressure release naturally. If desired, serve with additional green onions.

⅔ **CUP:** 209 cal., 8g fat (5g sat. fat), 20mg chol., 519mg sod., 30g carb. (2g sugars, 1g fiber), 4g pro. **DIABETIC EXCHANGES:** 2 starch, 2 fat.

ROSEMARY BEETS

We're a family of beet eaters. For a simple side, I use a one-dish cooker and let the beets mellow with rosemary and thyme.
—Nancy Heishman, Las Vegas, NV

Prep: 20 min. + cooling
Cook: 20 min. + releasing
Makes: 8 servings

- 5 **large fresh beets (about 3½ lbs.)**
- 1 **Tbsp. olive oil**
- 1 **medium red onion, chopped**
- 2 **garlic cloves, minced**
- 1 **medium orange, peeled and chopped**
- ⅓ **cup honey**
- ¼ **cup white balsamic vinegar**
- 1 **Tbsp. minced fresh rosemary or 1 tsp. dried rosemary, crushed**
- 2 **tsp. minced fresh thyme or ¾ tsp. dried thyme**
- ¾ **tsp. salt**
- ½ **tsp. Chinese five-spice powder**
- ½ **tsp. coarsely ground pepper**
- 1 **cup crumbled feta cheese**

1. Place trivet insert and 1 cup water in a 6-qt. electric pressure cooker. Scrub beets, trimming tops to 1 in.; set on trivet. Lock lid; close pressure-release valve. Adjust to pressure-cook on high for 20 minutes. Let pressure release naturally. Press cancel.

2. Remove beets and cool enough to handle. Remove trivet; discard cooking juices. Wipe pot clean. Peel and cut beets into wedges.

3. Select saute setting; adjust for medium heat. Add oil. When oil is hot, cook and stir red onion until crisp-tender, 4-5 minutes. Add garlic; cook 1 minute longer. Stir in orange, honey, vinegar, rosemary, thyme, salt, Chinese five-spice, pepper and beets; heat through. Press cancel. Serve warm, or refrigerate and serve cold. Serve with a slotted spoon; sprinkle with cheese.

¾ **CUP:** 200 cal., 4g fat (2g sat. fat), 8mg chol., 511mg sod., 37g carb. (31g sugars, 5g fiber), 6g pro. **DIABETIC EXCHANGES:** 2 vegetable, 1 starch, 1 fat.

BLACK-EYED PEAS WITH HAM

Here's a regional favorite I grew to love after moving to the South. You'll never want to eat canned black-eyed peas again! Serve the dish as a side with grilled chicken, or make it your main course and round out the meal with greens and cornbread.
—Tammie Merrill, Wake Forest, NC

Prep: 10 min.
Cook: 20 min. + releasing
Makes: 10 servings

- 1 pkg. (16 oz.) dried black-eyed peas
- 4 cups water
- 1 cup cubed fully cooked ham
- 1 medium onion, finely chopped
- 3 garlic cloves, minced
- 2 tsp. seasoned salt
- 1 tsp. pepper
  Thinly sliced green onions, optional

1. Rinse and sort the black-eyed peas. Transfer to a 6-qt. electric pressure cooker. Stir in water, ham, onion, garlic, seasoned salt and pepper. Lock lid; close pressure-release valve. Adjust to pressure-cook on high for 18 minutes. Let pressure release naturally for 10 minutes; quick-release any remaining pressure.

2. Serve with a slotted spoon. If desired, sprinkle with sliced green onions.

FREEZE OPTION: Freeze cooled pea mixture in freezer containers. To use, partially thaw in refrigerator overnight. Heat through in a saucepan, stirring occasionally and adding a little water if necessary.

¾ **CUP:** 76 cal., 1g fat (0 sat. fat), 8mg chol., 476mg sod., 11g carb. (2g sugars, 3g fiber), 7g pro. **DIABETIC EXCHANGES:** 1 starch.

CHICKPEA TAGINE

While traveling through Morocco, my wife and I fell in love with the complex flavors of the many tagines we tried, so we came up with this no-fuss dish. It's great alongside grilled fish, or add shredded cooked chicken in the last 10 minutes for a change-of-pace entree.
—Raymond Wyatt, West St. Paul, MN

Prep: 30 min.
Cook: 5 min.
Makes: 12 servings

- 2 Tbsp. olive oil
- 2 garlic cloves, minced
- 2 tsp. paprika
- 1 tsp. ground ginger
- 1 tsp. ground cumin
- ½ tsp. salt
- ¼ tsp. pepper
- ¼ tsp. ground cinnamon
- 1 small butternut squash (about 2 lbs.), peeled and cut into ½-in. cubes
- 2 medium zucchini, cut into ½-in. pieces
- 1 can (15 oz.) chickpeas or garbanzo beans, rinsed and drained
- 1 medium sweet red pepper, coarsely chopped
- 1 medium onion, coarsely chopped
- 12 dried apricots, halved
- ½ cup water
- 2 to 3 tsp. harissa chili paste
- 2 tsp. honey
- 1 can (14.5 oz.) crushed tomatoes, undrained
- ¼ cup chopped fresh mint leaves
  Plain Greek yogurt, optional

1. Select saute setting on a 6-qt. electric pressure cooker. Adjust for medium heat; add oil. When oil is hot, add garlic, paprika, ginger, cumin, salt, pepper and cinnamon; cook and stir until fragrant, about 1 minute. Press cancel.

2. Add squash, zucchini, chickpeas, red pepper, onion, apricot halves, water, harissa and honey. Lock lid; close pressure-release valve. Adjust to pressure-cook on high for 3 minutes. Quick-release pressure. Press cancel. Gently stir in tomatoes and mint; heat through.

3. If desired, top with yogurt and additional mint, olive oil and honey.

¾ **CUP:** 127 cal., 3g fat (0 sat. fat), 0 chol., 224mg sod., 23g carb. (9g sugars, 6g fiber), 4g pro. **DIABETIC EXCHANGES:** 1½ starch, ½ fat.

WHY YOU'LL LOVE IT...

"I never had tagine before, but this recipe intrigued me. It was delicious and so easy to make! We ate it over quinoa, and it was delicious! I will definitely make it again!"
—KATIE, TASTEOFHOME.COM

SMOKY WHITE BEANS & HAM

I had never made or even eaten this dish before meeting my husband. Now I make it at least once a week. I serve it with some homemade sweet cornbread. Delicious!
—Christine Duffy, Sturgis, KY

Prep: 15 min.
Cook: 30 min. + releasing
Makes: 10 servings

- 1 lb. dried great northern beans
- 3 smoked ham hocks (about 1½ lbs.)
- 3 cans (14½ oz. each) reduced-sodium chicken or beef broth
- 2 cups water
- 1 large onion, chopped
- 1 Tbsp. onion powder
- 1 Tbsp. garlic powder
- 2 tsp. pepper
  Thinly sliced green onions, optional

1. Rinse and sort beans. Transfer to a 6-qt. electric pressure cooker. Add the ham hocks. Stir in broth, water, onion and seasonings. Lock lid; close pressure-release valve. Adjust to pressure-cook on high for 30 minutes. Let the pressure release naturally for 10 minutes; quick-release any remaining pressure. Press cancel.

2. When cool enough to handle, remove meat from bones; cut ham into small pieces and return to pressure cooker. Serve with a slotted spoon. Sprinkle with green onions if desired.

⅔ **CUP:** 196 cal., 2g fat (0 sat. fat), 8mg chol., 594mg sod., 32g carb. (2g sugars, 10g fiber), 15g pro. **DIABETIC EXCHANGES:** 2 starch, 2 lean meat.

FISH, SEAFOOD & MEATLESS

Whether you enjoy pasta with clam sauce, stuffed peppers or fish fillets baked to perfection, you'll savor the fresh favorites that follow. Best of all, each pares down calories, fat and sodium while keeping the focus on flavor.

DEEP DIVE INTO FISH

Brush up on your vocabulary, then get cooking!

DRESSED FISH

Ready to cook; has been gutted and scaled. It still has its head and tail.

FILLETS

Come from the side of the fish and are boneless. They may or may not be skinless.

FLATFISH

Has both eyes on top of a flat body. Flounder, sole, turbot and halibut are flatfish. Generally, flatfish is sold as fillets; halibut is typically sold as steaks.

FRESHWATER FISH

Are from streams, rivers and freshwater lakes.

LEAN FISH

Has a low fat content—it can be as low as 2.5% fat. Lean fish has a delicate texture and mild flavor. Due to the low fat content, it can dry out easily during cooking and is best cooked with some liquid or fat. Cooking by steaming methods including pressure cooking is recommended. If it is basted during cooking, it can also be baked, broiled or grilled.

MEDIUM-FAT FISH

Has a fat content around 6%. Its texture is firmer than lean fish and it has a neutral flavor. This type of fish withstands high temperatures and can be pressure cooked, baked, broiled, grilled or pan-fried.

HIGH-FAT FISH

Has a fat content of more than 6% and can be as high as 50%. Due to the high fat content, these fish have a meaty texture and a rich flavor. These fish stay moist during cooking and are suitable for pressure cooking, baking, broiling or grilling.

PAN-DRESSED FISH

A dressed fish with the head and tail removed.

ROUNDFISH

Has a round body and eyes on both sides of its head. They are sold pan-dressed or dressed, and as steaks or fillets.

SALTWATER FISH

Fish from seas or oceans.

STEAKS

Cross sections of large roundfish containing part of the backbone; usually steaks are ½ to 1 in. thick.

WHOLE FISH

Need to be gutted and scaled before cooking.

HOW TO TEST DONENESS TEMPERATURE

Fish doneness varies by the type of fish being cooked.

- The USDA recommends an internal temperature of 145°. A general rule is to cook fish for 10 minutes per every inch of thickness, measured at the thickest area. Start checking for doneness about 2 minutes before the recommended cooking time, because overcooked fish becomes tough and dry.

- For fish fillets, insert a fork at an angle into the thickest portion of fish and gently part the meat. When it is opaque and flakes into sections, it's cooked completely. But if the fish is still translucent, it's undercooked.

- For whole fish, insert a fork along the backbone and the top fillet. The fish is done when the fillet lifts easily from the bones.

- For mahi mahi and swordfish, cook until the flesh just turns opaque.

- For fresh tuna, cook to medium-rare or until slightly pink in the center. Longer cooking reduces the flavor.

KEEP IT FRESH

WHEN BUYING FISH, LOOK FOR:
- Fresh fish fillets or steaks that are firm with moist-looking flesh that bounces back when pressed.
- Shiny, bright skin.
- Whole fish with clear eyes (not sunken or cloudy) and a firm body that is springy to the touch.
- Fish with a mild aroma.
- Frozen fish in packages that are frozen solid, tightly sealed and free of freezer burn and odor.
- An appropriate substitute if your market does not carry the type of fish you want. It's best to swap fish with one that has about the same fat content as the fish in the recipe: lean, medium-fat or high-fat.

GENERAL GUIDELINES FOR PURCHASE WEIGHT AND SERVINGS
- 1 lb. whole fish = 1 serving
- 1 lb. pan-dressed fish = 2 servings
- 1 lb. steaks or fillets = 3-4 servings

REFRIGERATOR DEFROSTING
- Place the package on a tray to catch any liquid or juices.
- Defrosting time will vary depending on the weight and the thickness of the package.
- For a 1-lb. package, allow at least 12 hours.

COLD WATER DEFROSTING
- Place the fish or seafood in a leakproof plastic bag and seal.
- Submerge the sealed bag in a pan or dish of cold tap water.
- Change the water every 30 minutes.
- Allow 1-2 hours of thawing time per pound.

KEEP FISH FRESH
Fish stays freshest when stored on ice. To keep it ice-cold without mess or damaging the fish's texture, place frozen gel packs or blue ice blocks in a container, then put the wrapped fish on top. Use within a few days. Always wash the ice packs with hot soapy water before reuse.

WHY CHOOSE A MEATLESS DIET?

PROTEIN HEALTH
A plant-based diet is typically antioxidant-rich, high in fiber and low in cholesterol. Many choose vegetarian food to reduce cholesterol and lower blood pressure; to help prevent many cancers such as colon, breast, stomach, esophageal, lung and prostate; and to help control diabetes.

WEIGHT LOSS
In a well-balanced vegetarian diet, weight loss is a possibility. However, like any other diet, a vegetarian diet high in calories from nuts, full-fat dairy and junk food may result in weight gain.

BUDGET
Forgoing meat and adding more economical staples, such as grains and dried legumes, can lower grocery bills.

RESPECT FOR LIFE
Many vegans feel that all living beings, including animals, have value, and they oppose using animals to serve any human need, whether for food, clothing, household goods or product testing.

ENVIRONMENTAL CONCERNS
Some people refrain from consuming meat to help the environment. They believe humans should eat grains or crops rather than using farmland to grow a vast quantity of grain or grass to feed animals, producing a smaller volume of animal protein. "Food animals" also create animal waste. A vegetarian diet helps reduce the planet's carbon footprint.

RELIGIOUS BELIEFS
Various religions have dietary guidelines that restrict the consumption of some kinds of meat or even all meat.

CHICKPEA & POTATO CURRY

I make chana masala, the classic Indian dish, in my one-pot cooker. Browning the onion, ginger and garlic first really makes the sauce amazing.
—Anjana Devasahayam, San Antonio, TX

Prep: 25 min.
Cook: 5 min. + releasing
Makes: 6 servings

- 1 Tbsp. canola oil
- 1 medium onion, chopped
- 2 garlic cloves, minced
- 2 tsp. minced fresh gingerroot
- 2 tsp. ground coriander
- 1 tsp. garam masala
- 1 tsp. chili powder
- ½ tsp. salt
- ½ tsp. ground cumin
- ¼ tsp. ground turmeric
- 2½ cups vegetable stock
- 2 cans (15 oz. each) chickpeas or garbanzo beans, rinsed and drained
- 1 can (15 oz.) crushed tomatoes
- 1 large baking potato, peeled and cut into ¾-in. cubes
- 1 Tbsp. lime juice
  Chopped fresh cilantro
  Hot cooked rice
  Optional: Sliced red onion and lime wedges

1. Select saute setting on a 6-qt. electric pressure cooker. Adjust for medium heat; add oil. When oil is hot, cook and stir onion until crisp-tender, 2-4 minutes. Add garlic, ginger and dry seasonings; cook and stir 1 minute. Add stock to pressure cooker. Cook 30 seconds, stirring to loosen browned bits from pan. Press cancel. Stir in chickpeas, tomatoes and potato.

2. Lock lid; close pressure-release valve. Adjust to pressure-cook on high for 3 minutes. Let pressure release naturally for 10 minutes; quick-release any remaining pressure.

3. Stir in lime juice; sprinkle with cilantro. Serve with rice and, if desired, red onion and lime wedges.

1¼ **CUPS:** 240 cal., 6g fat (0 sat. fat), 0 chol., 767mg sod., 42g carb. (8g sugars, 9g fiber), g pro.

DID YOU KNOW?
Garam masala is a rich blend of ground spices that often include peppercorns, cumin, coriander, fennel, cloves and cardamom. You can find garam masala in the spice aisle of most grocery stores.

STEAMED MUSSELS WITH PEPPERS

Here's a worthy way to use your Instant Pot. Serve French bread along with the mussels to soak up the deliciously seasoned broth. If you like your food spicy, add the jalapeno seeds.
—*Taste of Home* Test Kitchen

Prep: 30 min.
Cook: 5 min.
Makes: 4 servings

- 2 lbs. fresh mussels, scrubbed and beards removed
- 2 Tbsp. olive oil
- 1 jalapeno pepper, seeded and chopped
- 3 garlic cloves, minced
- 1 bottle (8 oz.) clam juice
- ½ cup white wine or additional clam juice
- ⅓ cup chopped sweet red pepper
- 3 green onions, sliced
- ½ tsp. dried oregano
- 1 bay leaf
- 2 Tbsp. minced fresh parsley
- ¼ tsp. salt
- ¼ tsp. pepper
  French bread baguette, sliced, optional

1. Tap mussels; discard any that do not close. Set aside. Select saute setting on a 6-qt. electric pressure cooker. Adjust for medium heat; add oil. When oil is hot, cook and stir chopped jalapeno until crisp-tender, 2-3 minutes. Add garlic; cook for 1 minute longer. Press cancel. Stir in mussels, clam juice, wine, red pepper, green onions, oregano and bay leaf. Lock lid; close pressure-release valve. Adjust to pressure-cook on high 2 minutes. Quick-release pressure.

2. Discard bay leaf and any unopened mussels. Sprinkle with parsley, salt and pepper. If desired, serve with baguette slices.

12 MUSSELS: 293 cal., 12g fat (2g sat. fat), 65mg chol., 931mg sod., 12g carb. (1g sugars, 1g fiber), 28g pro.

TEST KITCHEN TIP
Purchase mussels that are alive and fresh. Mussel shells should be damp and shiny, and they should smell like the ocean. For a more substantial serving, consider buying ¾ to 1 lb. mussels per person.

SPICE TRADE BEANS & BULGUR

A rich blend of treasured spices turn nutritious bulgur and chickpeas into a tangy stew with just the right amount of heat. I think the hint of sweetness from golden raisins makes a perfect accent.
—Faith Cromwell, San Francisco, CA

Prep: 30 min.
Cook: 15 min.
Makes: 10 servings

3 Tbsp. canola oil, divided
1½ cups bulgur
2 medium onions, chopped
1 medium sweet red pepper, chopped
5 garlic cloves, minced
1 Tbsp. ground cumin
1 Tbsp. paprika
2 tsp. ground ginger
1 tsp. pepper
½ tsp. ground cinnamon
½ tsp. cayenne pepper
1 carton (32 oz.) vegetable broth
2 Tbsp. soy sauce
1 can (28 oz.) crushed tomatoes
1 can (14½ oz.) diced tomatoes, undrained
1 can (15 oz.) garbanzo beans or chickpeas, rinsed and drained
½ cup golden raisins
2 Tbsp. brown sugar
Minced fresh cilantro, optional

1. Select saute setting on a 6-qt. electric pressure cooker. Adjust for medium heat; add 1 Tbsp. oil. When oil is hot, cook and stir bulgur until lightly browned, 2-3 minutes. Remove from pressure cooker.

2. Heat remaining 2 Tbsp. oil in pressure cooker. Cook and stir onions and red pepper until crisp-tender, 2-3 minutes. Add garlic and seasonings; cook 1 minute longer. Press cancel. Add broth, soy sauce and bulgur to pressure cooker.

3. Lock lid; close pressure-release valve. Adjust to pressure-cook on low for 12 minutes. Quick-release pressure. Press cancel. Select saute setting and adjust for low heat. Add the tomatoes, beans, raisins and brown sugar; simmer, uncovered, until mixture is slightly thickened and heated through, about 10 minutes, stirring occasionally. If desired, sprinkle with the minced cilantro.

1¼ CUPS: 245 cal., 6g fat (0 sat. fat), 0 chol., 752mg sod., 45g carb. (15g sugars, 8g fiber), 8g pro.

SIMPLE POACHED SALMON

I love this recipe because it's healthy and almost effortless. The salmon always cooks to perfection and is ready in hardly any time!
—Erin Chilcoat, Central Islip, NY

Prep: 10 min.
Cook: 5 min.
Makes: 4 servings

  2 **cups water**
  1 **cup white wine**
  1 **medium onion, sliced**
  1 **celery rib, sliced**
  1 **medium carrot, sliced**
  2 **Tbsp. lemon juice**
  3 **fresh thyme sprigs**
  1 **fresh rosemary sprig**
  1 **bay leaf**
  ½ **tsp. salt**
  ¼ **tsp. pepper**
  4 **salmon fillets (1¼ in. thick and 6 oz. each)**
     Lemon wedges

1. Combine the first 11 ingredients in a 6-qt. electric pressure cooker; top with salmon. Lock lid; close the pressure-release valve. Adjust to pressure cook on high for 3 minutes. Quick-release pressure. A thermometer inserted in fish should read at least 145°.

2. Remove fish from pressure cooker. Serve warm or cold with lemon wedges.

1 SALMON FILLET: 270 cal., 16g fat (3g sat. fat), 85mg chol., 115mg sod., 0 carb. (0 sugars, 0 fiber), 29g pro. **DIABETIC EXCHANGES:** 4 lean meat.

MANCHESTER STEW

While in college, I studied abroad. A vegetarian at the time, I was pleasantly surprised by how delicious and diverse vegetarian food in Britain could be. After returning to the States I re-created my favorite meal from my favorite restaurant and named it after the University of Manchester. When the enticing aroma fills the kitchen, I'm back in England!
—Kimberly Hammond, Kingwood, TX

Prep: 25 min.
Cook: 5 min. + releasing
Makes: 6 servings

- 2 Tbsp. olive oil
- 2 medium onions, chopped
- 2 garlic cloves, minced
- 1 tsp. dried oregano
- 1 cup dry red wine
- 1 lb. small red potatoes, quartered
- 1 can (16 oz.) kidney beans, rinsed and drained
- ½ lb. sliced fresh mushrooms
- 2 medium leeks (white portion only), sliced
- 1 cup fresh baby carrots
- 2½ cups water
- 1 can (14½ oz.) no-salt-added diced tomatoes
- 1 tsp. dried thyme
- ½ tsp. salt
- ¼ tsp. pepper
  Fresh basil leaves

1. Select saute setting on a 6-qt. electric pressure cooker. Adjust for medium heat; add oil. When oil is hot, cook and stir onions until crisp-tender, 2-3 minutes. Add garlic and oregano; cook and stir 1 minute longer. Stir in wine. Bring to a boil; cook until liquid is reduced by half, 3-4 minutes. Press cancel.

2. Add potatoes, beans, mushrooms, leeks and carrots. Stir in water, tomatoes, thyme, salt and pepper. Lock lid; close pressure-release valve. Adjust to pressure-cook on high for 3 minutes. Let pressure release naturally for 10 minutes; quick-release any remaining pressure. Top with basil leaves.

1⅔ **CUPS:** 221 cal., 5g fat (1g sat. fat), 0 chol., 354mg sod., 38g carb. (8g sugars, 8g fiber), 8g pro. **DIABETIC EXCHANGES:** 2 starch, 1 vegetable, 1 fat.

LENTIL STEW

This vegetarian stew is perfect when you want to take a little break from meat. Adding the cream at the end gives the dish a wonderfully smooth texture.
—Michelle Collins, Suffolk, VA

Prep: 45 min.
Cook: 15 min. + releasing
Makes: 8 servings (2¾ qt.)

- 2 Tbsp. canola oil
- 2 large onions, thinly sliced, divided
- 8 plum tomatoes, chopped
- 2 Tbsp. minced fresh gingerroot
- 3 garlic cloves, minced
- 2 tsp. ground coriander
- 1½ tsp. ground cumin
- ¼ tsp. cayenne pepper
- 3 cups vegetable broth
- 2 cups dried lentils, rinsed
- 2 cups water
- 1 can (4 oz.) chopped green chiles
- ¾ cup heavy whipping cream
- 2 Tbsp. butter
- 1 tsp. cumin seeds
- 6 cups hot cooked basmati or jasmine rice
  Optional: Sliced green onions or minced fresh cilantro

1. Select saute setting on a 6-qt. electric pressure cooker. Adjust for medium heat; add oil. When oil is hot, cook and stir half the onions until crisp-tender, 2-3 minutes. Add tomatoes, ginger and garlic, coriander, cumin and cayenne; cook and stir 1 minute longer. Press cancel. Stir in broth, lentils, water, green chiles and remaining onion.

2. Lock lid; close pressure-release valve. Adjust to pressure cook on high for 15 minutes. Let pressure release naturally. Just before serving, stir in the cream. In a small skillet, heat butter over medium heat. Add cumin seeds; cook and stir until golden brown, for 1-2 minutes. Add to lentil mixture.

3. Serve with rice. If desired, sprinkle with sliced green onions or minced cilantro.

1⅓ CUPS STEW WITH ¾ CUP RICE: 497 cal., 16g fat (8g sat. fat), 33mg chol., 345mg sod., 73g carb. (5g sugars, 8g fiber), 17g pro.

CLAM SAUCE

I serve this bright and fresh clam sauce often, usually with pasta; however, it's also delectable as a warm dip for special get-togethers.
—Frances Pietsch, Flower Mound, TX

Prep: 10 min.
Cook: 5 min.
Makes: 4 cups

4 Tbsp. butter
2 Tbsp. olive oil
½ cup finely chopped onion
8 oz. fresh mushrooms, chopped
2 garlic cloves, minced
2 cans (10 oz. each) whole baby clams
½ cup water
¼ cup sherry
2 tsp. lemon juice
1 bay leaf
¾ tsp. dried oregano
½ tsp. garlic salt
¼ tsp. white pepper
¼ tsp. Italian seasoning
¼ tsp. black pepper
2 Tbsp. chopped fresh parsley
Hot cooked pasta
Grated Parmesan cheese, additional lemon juice, minced parsley optional

1. Select saute setting on a 6-qt. electric pressure cooker. Adjust for medium heat; add butter and oil. When hot, cook and stir onion 2 minutes. Add mushrooms and garlic; cook 1 minute longer. Press cancel.

2. Drain clams, reserving liquid; coarsely chop. Add clams, reserved clam juice and the next 9 ingredients to pressure cooker. Lock lid; close pressure-release valve. Adjust to pressure-cook on high 2 minutes. Quick-release pressure.

3. Discard bay leaf; stir in parsley. Serve with pasta. If desired, serve with grated Parmesan cheese and additional lemon juice and parsley.

½ **CUP:** 138 cal., 10g fat (4g sat. fat), 40mg chol., 580mg sod., 5g carb. (1g sugars, 0 fiber), 7g pro.

TOMATO-POACHED HALIBUT

Simple halibut with a burst of lemon comes together easily. Serve it with bread or, even better, try it with polenta or angel hair pasta.
—Danna Rogers, Westport, CT

Prep: 15 min.
Cook: 5 min.
Makes: 4 servings

- 1 Tbsp. olive oil
- 2 poblano peppers, finely chopped
- 1 small onion, finely chopped
- 1 can (14½ oz.) fire-roasted diced tomatoes, undrained
- 1 can (14½ oz.) no-salt-added diced tomatoes, undrained
- ½ cup water
- ¼ cup chopped pitted green olives
- 3 garlic cloves, minced
- ¼ tsp. pepper
- ⅛ tsp. salt
- 4 halibut fillets (4 oz. each)
- ⅓ cup chopped fresh cilantro
- 4 lemon wedges
  Crusty whole grain bread, optional

1. Select saute setting on a 6-qt. electric pressure cooker. Adjust for medium heat; add oil. When oil is hot, cook and stir poblano peppers and onion until crisp-tender, 2-3 minutes. Press cancel. Stir in tomatoes, water, olives, garlic, pepper and salt. Top with fillets.

2. Lock the lid; close pressure-release valve. Adjust to pressure cook on high for 3 minutes. Quick-release pressure. A thermometer inserted in fish should read at least 145°.

3. Sprinkle with cilantro. Serve with lemon wedges and, if desired, bread.

1 FILLET WITH 1 CUP SAUCE: 215 cal., 7g fat (1g sat. fat), 56mg chol., 614mg sod., 16g carb. (7g sugars, 3g fiber), 23g pro. **DIABETIC EXCHANGES:** 3 lean meat, 1 starch, ½ fat.

FISH STEW

I love fish and chowder, so this stew is a favorite of mine. It's made without cream or whole milk so I don't have to worry about extra fat or calories.
—Jane Whittaker, Pensacola, FL

Prep: 25 min.
Cook: 5 min. + releasing
Makes: 8 servings (3 qt.)

- 1 lb. potatoes (about 2 medium), peeled and finely chopped
- 1 can (14½ oz.) diced tomatoes, undrained
- 1 can (10½ oz.) condensed cream of celery soup, undiluted
- 1 pkg. (10 oz.) frozen corn, thawed
- 1½ cups frozen lima beans, thawed
- 1½ cups vegetable or chicken broth
- 1 large onion, finely chopped
- 1 celery rib, finely chopped
- 1 medium carrot, finely chopped
- ½ cup white wine or additional vegetable broth
- 4 garlic cloves, minced
- 1 bay leaf
- 1 tsp. lemon-pepper seasoning
- 1 tsp. dried parsley flakes
- 1 tsp. dried rosemary, crushed
- ½ tsp. salt
- 1 lb. cod fillets, cut into 1-in. pieces
- 1 can (12 oz.) fat-free evaporated milk

1. Combine the first 16 ingredients in a 6-qt. electric pressure cooker; top with cod. Lock lid; close pressure-release valve. Adjust to pressure-cook on high for 2 minutes.

2. Let pressure release naturally. Discard bay leaf. Stir in milk until heated through.

1½ **CUPS:** 233 cal., 3g fat (1g sat. fat), 25mg chol., 701mg sod., 36g carb. (11g sugars, 5g fiber), 18g pro. **DIABETIC EXCHANGES:** 2 starch, 2 lean meat.

TEST KITCHEN TIP
Feel free to try this recipe with a pound of any variety fish fillets. Just be sure the fish is cut into 1-in. pieces for even cooking.

STUFFED PEPPERS

Here's a good-for-you dinner that's also a meatless meal-in-one classic. Add a salad and in just moments, the family will be running to the table.
—Michelle Gurnsey, Lincoln, NE

Prep: 15 min.
Cook: 5 min. + releasing
Makes: 4 servings

- 4 **medium sweet red peppers**
- 1 **can (15 oz.) black beans, rinsed and drained**
- 1 **cup shredded pepper jack cheese**
- ¾ **cup salsa**
- 1 **small onion, chopped**
- ½ **cup frozen corn**
- ⅓ **cup uncooked converted long grain rice**
- 1¼ **tsp. chili powder**
- ½ **tsp. ground cumin**
  Reduced-fat sour cream, optional

1. Place trivet insert and 1 cup water in a 6-qt. electric pressure cooker.

2. Cut and discard tops from peppers; remove seeds. In a large bowl, mix beans, cheese, salsa, onion, corn, rice, chili powder and cumin; spoon into peppers. Set peppers on trivet.

3. Lock lid; close pressure-release valve. Adjust to pressure-cook on high for 5 minutes. Let pressure release naturally. If desired, serve with sour cream.

1 STUFFED PEPPER: 333 cal., 10g fat (5g sat. fat), 30mg chol., 582mg sod., 45g carb. (8g sugars, 8g fiber), 15g pro. **DIABETIC EXCHANGES:** 2 starch, 2 lean meat, 2 vegetable, 1 fat.

WHY YOU'LL LOVE IT...

"This is one of my favorite vegetarian dishes! My family loves it! So glad I discovered this dish! Thank you!"
—LOURENA, TASTEOFHOME.COM

PORK DINNERS

When it comes to lighter meals, pork is a natural choice. Whether you're looking for a quick weeknight supper or an impressive entree for weekend guests, pork offers the versatility, ease and flavor today's cooks crave.

GUIDE TO PORK

When it comes to serving up meals that are lean, tender and satisfying, pork is a natural choice. Find new ways to serve ribs, roasts, chops, ham and more.

PORK PURCHASING GUIDELINES

- Pork with firm meat, a pink color and a small amount of fat on the surface.

- A package with no holes, tears or excess liquid, which may indicate improper handling and storage.

- A sell-by date on the package that is later than the day of your purchase. If it is the same date, use the meat that day or freeze it for later.

- For the leanest pork options, opt for any cut of loin.

GENERAL GUIDELINES FOR PORK PURCHASE WEIGHT AND SERVINGS

- 4 oz. of uncooked, boneless pork = 3 oz. cooked serving

- 1 lb. of any boneless cuts = 4 servings

- 1 lb. bone-in roasts, chops or ham = 2½-3 servings

- 1 lb. spareribs = about 1¼ servings

HOW LEAN IS PORK?

Some of the leanest cuts of pork are boneless loin roasts or chops, boneless sirloin roasts or chops, and bone-in pork loin chops. Ounce for ounce, pork tenderloin is as lean as boneless skinless chicken breast.

QUICK & VERSATILE

Considering which cut of pork to use will help set a meal on the table quicker. For instance, lean pork tenderloin can be grilled in less than half an hour. Cut it into medallions or cutlets, pork makes super-fast stovetop entrees. Don't forget about chops, such as ½-in.-thick rib or loin chops. Cooked on the stovetop, they can be ready in a flash. And for stir-fries or pork strips make a delicious choice.

To make sure pork is done and safe to eat, consider these basic guidelines:

- Whole cuts of fresh pork are safe when cooked to 145° with a 3-5 minute rest time.

- If you like a firmer texture, cook pork to temperatures above 145°.

- Cook ground pork to a minimum of 160°.

▶ **MEDIUM-RARE**
145-150°F

▶ **MEDIUM**
150-155°F

▶ **MEDIUM-WELL**
155-160°F

▶ **WELL**
160°F

PORK DONENESS PHOTO COURTESY OF
NATIONAL PORK BOARD DES MOINES, IOWA USA

PORK DINNERS MADE EASY

Planning a healthy meal is a snap when pork plays a starring role on the menu. Use this chart for compatible menu ideas when you are looking to round out the main courses in this chapter.

PORK RECIPE
Pork Chops,
Page 110

MENU ADD-ONS
- Sweet potatoes
- Sugar-free iced tea

PORK RECIPE
Pork Chops & Acorn Squash,
Page 114

MENU ADD-ONS
- Vegetable soup
- Bran muffins

PORK RECIPE
Mushroom Pork Ragout,
Page 113

MENU ADD-ONS
- Spinach salad
- Lemon sherbet

PORK RECIPE
Spicy Pork & Squash Ragu,
Page 117

MENU ADD-ONS
- Fruit salad
- Broiled eggplant

PORK RECIPE
Pork & Apple Curry,
Page 118

MENU ADD-ONS
- Whole grain naan
- Green tea

PORK RECIPE
Sweet Onion & Cherry
Pork Chops, Page 121

MENU ADD-ONS
- Steamed green beans
- Sugar-free vanilla pudding

PORK RECIPE
Pork Satay with
Rice Noodles, Page 122

MENU ADD-ONS
- Cucumber salad
- Fortune cookies

PORK RECIPE
Teriyaki Pork Roast,
Page 125

MENU ADD-ONS
- Roasted Brussels sprouts
- Brown rice

PORK RECIPE
Red Beans & Rice,
Page 126

MENU ADD-ONS
- Baked tortilla chips
- Salsa

PORK RECIPE
Pork Tacos with
Mango Salsa, Page 129

MENU ADD-ONS
- Grilled corn
- Fat-free refried beans

PORK RECIPE
Pork with Prunes and
Apples, Page 130

MENU ADD-ONS
- Wild rice
- Roasted asparagus

PORK CUTS

Know your pork! Consider this at-a-glance guide when deciding which cut makes the most sense for your family favorites.

▶ TENDER   ▶ LESS TENDER

PIG DIAGRAM LABELS: SHOULDER · LOIN · LEG · PICNIC · SIDE

▲ **SHOULDER**
BLADE STEAK

▶ **SHOULDER**
SHOULDER ARM PORK
ROAST, BONE-IN

▲ **LOIN**
BACK RIBS,
BABY

▲ **PICNIC**
PICNIC
SHOULDER

▲ **LOIN**
PORK
TENDERLOIN

▲ **LOIN**
COUNTRY-STYLE
SPARERIBS

▲ **SHOULDER**
BLADE ROAST,
BONELESS

▲ **LOIN**
PORK TOP LOIN
CHOP, NEW YORK

◀ **LOIN**
BONELESS
SIRLOIN
ROAST

◀ **SHOULDER**
GROUND
PORK

◀ **LOIN**
SIRLOIN CHOP

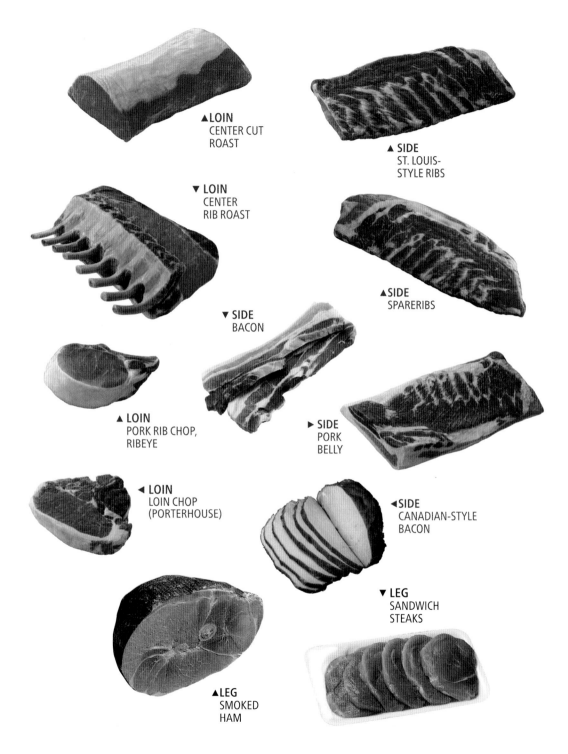

▲LOIN
CENTER CUT
ROAST

▲ SIDE
ST. LOUIS-
STYLE RIBS

▼ LOIN
CENTER
RIB ROAST

▲SIDE
SPARERIBS

▼ SIDE
BACON

▲ LOIN
PORK RIB CHOP,
RIBEYE

► SIDE
PORK
BELLY

◄ LOIN
LOIN CHOP
(PORTERHOUSE)

◄SIDE
CANADIAN-STYLE
BACON

▼ LEG
SANDWICH
STEAKS

▲LEG
SMOKED
HAM

PORK CHOPS

Everyone will enjoy these fork-tender pork chops with a creamy gravy...and no one will suspect they're eating light! Serve the chops with a green vegetable or a salad.
—Sue Bingham, Madisonville, TN

Prep: 15 min.
Cook: 5 min.
Makes: 4 servings

½ **cup all-purpose flour, divided**
½ **tsp. ground mustard**
½ **tsp. garlic-pepper blend**
¼ **tsp. seasoned salt**
4 **boneless pork loin chops (4 oz. each)**
2 **Tbsp. canola oil**
1 **can (14½ oz.) chicken broth, divided**

1. In a shallow bowl, mix ¼ cup flour, mustard, garlic pepper and seasoned salt. Add 1 pork chop at a time, and toss to coat; shake off excess.

2. Select saute or browning setting on a 6-qt. electric pressure cooker. Adjust for medium heat; add canola oil. When oil is hot, brown pork in batches. Add 1½ cups broth to pressure cooker. Cook for 30 seconds, stirring to loosen browned bits from pan. Press cancel. Return all to pressure cooker.

3. Lock lid; close pressure-release valve. Adjust to pressure-cook on high for 3 minutes. Quick-release pressure. A thermometer inserted in pork should read at least 145°. Press cancel. Remove pork to serving plate and keep warm.

4. In a small bowl, mix remaining ¼ cup flour and ¼ cup broth until smooth; stir into pressure cooker. Select saute setting and adjust for low heat. Simmer, stirring constantly, until thickened, 1-2 minutes. Serve with pork.

1 PORK CHOP WITH ⅓ CUP GRAVY: 257 cal., 14g fat (3g sat. fat), 57mg chol., 606mg sod., 8g carb. (0 sugars, 0 fiber), 23g pro. **DIABETIC EXCHANGES:** 3 lean meat, 1½ fat, ½ starch.

MUSHROOM PORK RAGOUT

This savory pork for two comes together quickly with a tomato gravy and noodles. It's a nice change from regular pork roast. I serve it with broccoli or green beans on the side.
—Connie McDowell, Greenwood, DE

Prep: 20 min.
Cook: 10 min.
Makes: 2 servings

- 1 **pork tenderloin (¾ lb.)**
- ⅛ **tsp. salt**
- ⅛ **tsp. pepper**
- 1½ **cups sliced fresh mushrooms**
- ¾ **cup canned crushed tomatoes**
- ¾ **cup reduced-sodium chicken broth, divided**
- ⅓ **cup sliced onion**
- 1 **Tbsp. chopped sun-dried tomatoes (not packed in oil)**
- 1¼ **tsp. dried savory**
- 1 **Tbsp. cornstarch**
- 1½ **cups hot cooked egg noodles**

1. Rub pork with salt and pepper; cut in half. Place in a 6-qt. electric pressure cooker. Top with mushrooms, tomatoes, ½ cup broth, onion, sun-dried tomatoes and savory.

2. Lock lid; close pressure-release valve. Adjust to pressure-cook on high for 6 minutes. Quick-release pressure. A thermometer inserted in pork should read at least 145°. Press cancel.

3. Remove pork; keep warm. In a small bowl, mix cornstarch and remaining broth until smooth; stir into pressure cooker. Select saute setting and adjust for low heat. Simmer, stirring constantly, until thickened, 1-2 minutes. Slice pork; serve with sauce and noodles.

FREEZE OPTION: Place sliced pork and vegetables in freezer containers; top with sauce. Cool and freeze. To use, partially thaw in refrigerator overnight. Heat through in a covered saucepan, stirring gently and adding a little broth if necessary.

1 SERVING: 387 cal., 8g fat (2g sat. fat), 119mg chol., 613mg sod., 37g carb. (8g sugars, 4g fiber), 43g pro. **DIABETIC EXCHANGES:** 5 lean meat, 2 vegetable, 1 starch.

PORK CHOPS & ACORN SQUASH

My husband and I are crazy for the squash we grow in our garden. For a sweet and tangy dish, we pressure-cook it with pork chops and orange juice.
—Mary Johnson, Coloma, WI

Prep: 15 min.
Cook: 5 min.
Makes: 6 servings

- 6 **boneless pork loin chops (4 oz. each)**
- 2 **medium acorn squash, halved lengthwise, seeded and sliced**
- ½ **cup packed brown sugar**
- ½ **cup reduced-sodium chicken broth**
- 2 **Tbsp. butter, melted**
- 1 **Tbsp. orange juice**
- ¾ **tsp. salt**
- ¾ **tsp. browning sauce, optional**
- ½ **tsp. grated orange zest**

Place the pork chops in a 6-qt. electric pressure cooker; add squash. In a small bowl, mix the remaining ingredients; pour over squash. Lock lid; close pressure-release valve. Adjust to pressure-cook on high for 4 minutes. Quick-release pressure. A thermometer inserted in pork should read at least 145°.

1 SERVING: 349 cal., 11g fat (5g sat. fat), 65mg chol., 416mg sod., 42g carb. (23g sugars, 3g fiber), 24g pro.

TEST KITCHEN TIP
Select acorn squash that feel heavy for their size and are free of blemishes and cuts. The skin should be dark and glossy.

SPICY PORK & SQUASH RAGU

This recipe is a marvelously spicy combo perfect for cooler weather. It's so satisfying after a day spent outdoors.
—Monica Osterhaus, Paducah, KY

Prep: 20 min.
Cook: 15 min. + releasing
Makes: 10 servings

- 2 **cans (14½ oz. each) stewed tomatoes, undrained**
- 1 **pkg. (12 oz.) frozen cooked winter squash, thawed**
- 1 **large sweet onion, cut into ½-in. pieces**
- 1 **medium sweet red pepper, cut into ½-in. pieces**
- ¾ **cup reduced-sodium chicken broth**
- 1½ **tsp. crushed red pepper flakes**
- 2 **lbs. boneless country-style pork ribs**
- 1 **tsp. salt**
- ¼ **tsp. garlic powder**
- ¼ **tsp. pepper**
  Hot cooked pasta
  Shaved Parmesan cheese, optional

1. Combine first 6 ingredients in a 6-qt. electric pressure cooker. Sprinkle ribs with salt, garlic powder and pepper; place in pressure cooker. Lock lid; close pressure-release valve. Adjust to pressure-cook on high for 15 minutes. Let pressure release naturally for 10 minutes; quick-release any remaining pressure.

2. Remove cover; stir to break pork into smaller pieces. Serve with pasta. If desired, top with Parmesan cheese.

FREEZE OPTION: Freeze cooled sauce in freezer containers. To use, partially thaw in refrigerator overnight. Heat through in a saucepan, stirring occasionally.

1 CUP RAGU: 196 cal., 8g fat (3g sat. fat), 52mg chol., 469mg sod., 13g carb. (6g sugars, 2g fiber), 18g pro. **DIABETIC EXCHANGES:** 2 lean meat, 1 starch.

PORK & APPLE CURRY

Here's a gentle curry dish that's won't overwhelm more delicate palates. For fun, try varying the garnish—add a few chopped peanuts or a little chutney, for instance.
—Nancy Reck, Mill Valley, CA

Prep: 15 min.
Cook: 10 min.
Makes: 8 servings

- 2 lbs. boneless pork loin roast, cut into 1-in. cubes
- 1 small onion, chopped
- ½ cup orange juice
- 1 Tbsp. curry powder
- 1 tsp. chicken bouillon granules
- 1 garlic clove, minced
- ½ tsp. salt
- ½ tsp. ground ginger
- ¼ tsp. ground cinnamon
- 1 medium apple, peeled and chopped
- 2 Tbsp. cornstarch
- 2 Tbsp. cold water
   Hot cooked rice, optional
- ¼ cup raisins
- ¼ cup sweetened shredded coconut, toasted

1. In a 6-qt. electric pressure cooker, combine the first 9 ingredients. Lock lid; close pressure-release valve. Adjust to pressure-cook on high for 3 minutes. Quick-release the pressure. A thermometer inserted in pork should read at least 145°. Press cancel.

2. Add apple to pressure cooker. In a small bowl, combine cornstarch and water until smooth; stir into pressure cooker. Select saute setting and adjust for low heat. Simmer, stirring constantly, until thickened and apple is tender, 3-5 minutes.

3. If desired, serve with rice. Sprinkle with raisins and coconut.

⅔ **CUP:** 174 cal., 6g fat (2g sat. fat), 57mg chol., 287mg sod., 8g carb. (4g sugars, 1g fiber), 22g pro. **DIABETIC EXCHANGES:** 3 lean meat, ½ starch.

WHY YOU'LL LOVE IT...

"Pork and apple curry is one my family simply loves and makes any time we can. It's usually served over rice, which is just fine with all of us, as we love rice dishes."
—TKARINAS, TASTEOFHOME.COM

SWEET ONION & CHERRY PORK CHOPS

When I want to jump-start supper, I opt for these tender pork chops. The sweet and savory cherry sauce makes this recipe a keeper. Try serving it with wild rice pilaf.
—Stephanie Ray, Naples, FL

Prep: 15 min.
Cook: 5 min.
Makes: 4 servings

- 1 **cup fresh or frozen pitted tart cherries, thawed**
- 1 **cup reduced-sodium chicken broth**
- ¼ **cup chopped sweet onion**
- 2 **Tbsp. honey**
- 1 **tsp. seasoned salt**
- ½ **tsp. pepper**
- 4 **boneless pork loin chops (5 oz. each)**
- 1 **Tbsp. cornstarch**
- 1 **Tbsp. cold water**

1. In a 6-qt. electric pressure cooker, combine the first 6 ingredients; top with pork chops. Lock lid; close pressure-release valve. Adjust to pressure-cook on high for 3 minutes. Quick-release pressure. A thermometer inserted in pork should read at least 145°. Press cancel.

2. Remove pork to a serving platter; keep warm. In a small bowl, mix cornstarch and water until smooth; stir into the pressure cooker. Select saute setting and adjust for low heat. Simmer, stirring constantly, until thickened, 1-2 minutes. Serve with pork.

1 PORK CHOP WITH ¼ CUP CHERRY MIXTURE: 259 cal., 8g fat (3g sat. fat), 68mg chol., 567mg sod., 17g carb. (14g sugars, 1g fiber), 29g pro. **DIABETIC EXCHANGES:** 4 lean meat, 1 starch, ½ fat.

PORK SATAY WITH RICE NOODLES

I love the addition of peanuts to savory recipes. Intensify the flavor by sprinkling with minced fresh cilantro and chopped peanuts for that restaurant-quality look and taste.
—Stephanie Anderson, Horseheads, NY

Prep: 20 min.
Cook: 5 min.
Makes: 6 servings

- 1½ lbs. boneless pork loin chops, cut into 2-in. pieces
- ¼ tsp. pepper
- 1 medium onion, halved and sliced
- ⅓ cup creamy peanut butter
- ¼ cup reduced-sodium soy sauce
- ½ tsp. onion powder
- ½ tsp. garlic powder
- ½ tsp. hot pepper sauce
- 1 can (14½ oz.) reduced-sodium chicken broth, divided
- 3 Tbsp. cornstarch
- 9 oz. uncooked thick rice noodles
  Optional: Minced fresh cilantro and chopped peanuts

1. Sprinkle pork with pepper. Place in a 6-qt. electric pressure cooker; top with onion. In a small bowl, mix peanut butter, soy sauce, onion powder, garlic powder and pepper sauce; gradually add 1½ cups broth. Pour over onion.

2. Lock the lid; close pressure-release valve. Adjust to pressure-cook on high for 3 minutes. Quick-release pressure. A thermometer inserted in pork should read at least 145°. Press cancel. Remove pork chops from pressure cooker and keep warm.

3. In a small bowl, mix cornstarch and remaining ¼ cup broth until smooth; stir into pressure cooker. Select saute setting and adjust for low heat. Simmer, stirring constantly, until thickened, 1-2 minutes. Add pork; heat through.

4. Meanwhile, cook rice noodles according to package directions; drain. Serve with pork mixture. If desired, sprinkle with cilantro and peanuts.

1 SERVING: 427 cal., 14g fat (4g sat. fat), 55mg chol., 754mg sod., 44g carb. (3g sugars, 2g fiber), 29g pro.

TERIYAKI PORK ROAST

I'm always looking for no-fuss recipes, so I was thrilled to find this one. The tender teriyaki pork has become a family favorite.
—Roxanne Hulsey, Gainesville, GA

Prep: 10 min.
Cook: 30 min. + releasing
Makes: 10 servings

- ¾ **cup unsweetened apple juice**
- 2 **Tbsp. sugar**
- 2 **Tbsp. reduced-sodium soy sauce**
- 1 **Tbsp. white vinegar**
- 1 **tsp. ground ginger**
- ¼ **tsp. garlic powder**
- ⅛ **tsp. pepper**
- 1 **boneless pork loin roast (about 3 lbs.), halved**
- 8 **tsp. cornstarch**
- 3 **Tbsp. cold water**

1. Combine the first 7 ingredients in a 6-qt. electric pressure cooker. Add roast and turn to coat. Lock lid; close pressure-release valve. Adjust to pressure-cook on high for 25 minutes. Let pressure release naturally for 10 minutes; quick-release any remaining pressure. A thermometer inserted in pork should read at least 145°. Press cancel.

2. Remove pork to a serving platter; keep warm. In a small bowl, mix the cornstarch and water until smooth; stir into pressure cooker. Select saute setting and adjust for low heat. Simmer, stirring constantly, until thickened, 1-2 minutes. Serve with the pork.

FREEZE OPTION: Place sliced pork roast in freezer containers; top with sauce. Cool and freeze. To use, partially thaw in refrigerator overnight. Heat through in a covered saucepan, stirring gently and adding a little water if necessary.

4 OZ. COOKED PORK: 198 cal., 6g fat (2g sat. fat), 68mg chol., 155mg sod., 7g carb. (4g sugars, 0 fiber), 27g pro. **DIABETIC EXCHANGES:** 4 lean meat, ½ starch.

RED BEANS & RICE

My family loves New Orleans-style cooking, so I make this dish often. I appreciate how simple it is, and the smoky ham flavor is scrumptious.
—Celinda Dahlgren, Napa, CA

Prep: 20 min.
Cook: 45 min. + releasing
Makes: 6 servings

   3 cups water
   2 smoked ham hocks
      (about 1 lb.)
   1 cup dried red beans
   1 medium onion,
      chopped
1½ tsp. minced garlic
   1 tsp. ground cumin
   1 medium tomato,
      chopped
   1 medium green
      pepper, chopped
   1 tsp. salt
   4 cups hot cooked rice

1. Place the first 6 ingredients in a 6-qt. electric pressure cooker. Lock lid; close pressure-release valve. Adjust to pressure-cook on high for 35 minutes.

2. Let pressure release naturally. Press cancel. Remove ham hocks; cool slightly. Remove meat from bones. Finely chop meat and return to pressure cooker; discard bones. Stir in the tomato, green pepper and salt. Select saute setting and adjust for low heat. Simmer, stirring constantly, until pepper is tender, 8-10 minutes. Serve with rice.

FREEZE OPTION: Freeze cooled bean mixture in freezer containers. To use, partially thaw in refrigerator overnight. Microwave, covered, on high in a microwave-safe dish until heated through, gently stirring and adding a little water if necessary.

⅔ CUP BEAN MIXTURE WITH ⅔ CUP RICE: 216 cal., 2g fat (0 sat. fat), 9mg chol., 671mg sod., 49g carb. (3g sugars, 12g fiber), 12g pro.

PORK TACOS WITH MANGO SALSA

I've made quite a few tacos in my day, but you can't beat the tender filling made in a pressure cooker. These are by far the best pork tacos we've had—and we've tried plenty. Make the mango salsa from scratch if you have time!
—Amber Massey, Argyle, TX

Prep: 25 min.
Cook: 5 min.
Makes: 12 servings

- 2 Tbsp. white vinegar
- 2 Tbsp. lime juice
- 3 cups cubed fresh pineapple
- 1 small red onion, coarsely chopped
- 3 Tbsp. chili powder
- 2 chipotle peppers in adobo sauce
- 2 tsp. ground cumin
- 1½ tsp. salt
- ½ tsp. pepper
- 1 bottle (12 oz.) dark Mexican beer
- 3 lbs. pork tenderloin, cut into 1-in. cubes
- ¼ cup chopped fresh cilantro
- 1 jar (16 oz.) mango salsa
- 24 corn tortillas (6 in.), warmed
  Optional toppings: Cubed fresh pineapple, cubed avocado and queso fresco

1. Puree the first 9 ingredients in a blender; stir in beer. In a 6-qt. electric pressure cooker, combine pork and pineapple mixture. Lock the lid; close pressure-release valve. Adjust to pressure-cook on high for 3 minutes. Quick-release pressure. A thermometer inserted into pork should read at least 145°. Stir to break up pork.

2. Stir cilantro into salsa. Using a slotted spoon, serve pork mixture in tortillas; add salsa and toppings as desired.

FREEZE OPTION: Freeze cooled meat mixture and cooking juices in freezer containers. To use, partially thaw in refrigerator overnight. Heat through in a saucepan, stirring occasionally.

2 TACOS: 284 cal., 6g fat (2g sat. fat), 64mg chol., 678mg sod., 30g carb. (5g sugars, 5g fiber), 26g pro. **DIABETIC EXCHANGES:** 3 lean meat, 2 starch.

WHY YOU'LL LOVE IT...

"This was so easy to prepare, and it was super good. The leftovers in the freezer will be so good. Meat was very tender and the blend of the spices was just perfect."
—BONITO15, TASTEOFHOME.COM

PORK WITH PRUNES & APPLES

The classic flavors of herbes de Provence, apples and dried plums make this easy entree taste like a hearty meal at a French country cafe. For a truly traditional meal, serve the pork with braised lentils.
—Suzanne Banfield, Basking Ridge, NJ

Prep: 20 min. + standing
Cook: 35 min. + releasing
Makes: 10 servings

- 1 **boneless pork loin roast (3 to 4 lbs.)**
- 2 **Tbsp. all-purpose flour**
- 1 **Tbsp. herbes de Provence**
- 1½ **tsp. salt**
- ¾ **tsp. pepper**
- 2 **Tbsp. olive oil**
- 1 **cup apple cider or unsweetened apple juice**
- 2 **medium onions, halved and thinly sliced**
- 1 **cup beef stock**
- 2 **bay leaves**
- 2 **large tart apples, peeled and chopped**
- 1 **cup pitted dried plums**

1. Halve roast. Mix flour, herbes de Provence, salt and pepper; rub over pork. Select saute or browning setting on a 6-qt. electric pressure cooker. Adjust for medium heat; add 1 Tbsp. oil. When oil is hot, brown a roast half on all sides. Remove; repeat with remaining pork and oil.

2. Add cider to pressure cooker. Cook 1 minute, stirring to loosen browned bits from pan. Press cancel. Add onions, stock, bay leaves and roast.

3. Lock lid; close pressure-release valve. Adjust to pressure-cook on high for 25 minutes. Let pressure release naturally for 10 minutes; quick-release any remaining pressure. A thermometer inserted in pork should read at least 145°. Press cancel. Remove roast and onions to a serving platter, discarding bay leaves; tent with foil.

4. Select saute setting and adjust for low heat. Add apples and plums; simmer, uncovered, until the apples are tender, 6-8 minutes, stirring occasionally. Serve with roast.

4 OZ. COOKED PORK WITH ¾ CUP FRUIT MIXTURE: 286 cal., 9g fat (3g sat. fat), 68mg chol., 449mg sod., 22g carb. (13g sugars, 2g fiber), 28g pro.

POULTRY FAVORITES

Chicken and turkey save the day whenever time is tight, particularly when your one-pot cooker is in the mix. Consider these full-flavored entrees when you're watching the clock and the scale.

PICKING THE RIGHT POULTRY

When purchasing chicken and turkey, be sure you understand your options.

BASTED OR SELF-BASTED
Chicken or turkey that has been injected or marinated with a solution of water, broth or stock that contains some form of fat, such as butter, plus spices and flavor enhancers.

BROILER/FRYER
A chicken about 7 weeks old that weighs 2½-4½ pounds.

CAPON
A castrated male chicken between 4 and 8 months old that weighs 4-7 pounds.

CHICKEN LEG
The attached drumstick and thigh.

CHICKEN QUARTER
A quarter of the chicken, which may be the leg or breast quarter. The leg quarter contains the drumstick, thigh and portion of the back. The breast quarter contains the breast, wing and portion of the back.

CORNISH GAME HEN
A small broiler/fryer that is less than 30 days old and weighs 1¼-1½ pounds.

CUT-UP CHICKEN
A broiler/fryer that has been cut into two breast halves, two thighs, two drumsticks and two wings. It may or may not have the back.

DRUMMETTE
First section of a chicken wing.

DRUMSTICK
The lower portion of the leg.

FREE-RANGE OR FREE-ROAMING
The poultry was not confined to a chicken house but was allowed outside to forage for food.

FRESH POULTRY
Uncooked poultry that has never been commercially stored below 26°.

GIBLETS
The heart, liver, neck and gizzard.

HEN OR TOM TURKEY
Indicates whether the turkey was female (hen) or male (tom). Tom turkeys are usually larger than hen turkeys. They are equally tender.

HERITAGE TURKEY
These turkey breeds were developed over hundreds of years across the U.S. and Europe, and they're identified in the American Poultry Association's Turkey Standard of Perfection of 1874. Heritage turkeys take longer to raise and are more expensive. Cooks seek them out for their richer flavor and moister meat.

NATURAL
This label means the product does not contain artificial flavors, colors, chemical preservatives or other artificial or synthetic ingredients.

ORGANIC
The poultry was raised by a producer certified by the National Organic Program in compliance with USDA organic regulations.

ROASTER
A chicken between 3 and 5 months old that weighs 5-7 pounds.

SPLIT CHICKEN
A broiler/fryer that has been cut in half lengthwise.

HANDY AT-A-GLANCE HINTS

WHEN BUYING, LOOK FOR:

- Fresh, moist meat. The skin color of chicken ranges from white to deep yellow. Color is an indication of the chicken's diet, not freshness.

- Duck and goose in the freezer case. The holiday season is usually the best time to find them fresh.

- A package with no holes, tears or excessive liquid, which may indicate improper handling and storage.

- A sell-by date on the package that is later than the day of your purchase. If it is the same date, use the meat that day or freeze it for later.

REFRIGERATOR DEFROSTING:

- Place a tray under the meat to catch any liquid.

- Defrosting time will vary depending on the weight and thickness of the poultry.

- For bone-in parts or a small whole chicken, allow at least 1-2 days.

- For duck or goose parts, allow at least 1 day.

- For a whole duck or goose, allow at least 2 days.

- For a whole turkey or large whole chicken, allow 24 hours for every 4 pounds.

DONENESS TEMPERATURES AS MEASURED WITH A FOOD THERMOMETER:

165° Ground chicken and ground turkey

165° Chicken and turkey boneless breast minimum temperature

165° Stuffing

170° Chicken and turkey bone-in breast

170° Chicken and turkey boneless thighs

170°-175° Whole chicken and turkey as measured in thickest part of thigh

170°-175° Chicken and turkey legs, drumsticks and bone-in thighs

180° Duck, goose, pheasant

TYPE OF POULTRY	SERVINGS PER POUND
CHICKEN, WHOLE	1-2
CHICKEN PARTS (BONE-IN, SKIN-ON)	2-3
CHICKEN BREASTS (BONELESS SKINLESS)	3-4
TURKEY, WHOLE (12 LBS. OR LESS)	1
TURKEY, WHOLE (12 LBS. OR MORE)	2
TURKEY PARTS (THIGHS, BONE-IN BREASTS)	2-3
TURKEY BREAST (BONELESS)	3-4
DUCK, WHOLE	1
GOOSE, WHOLE	1
CORNISH GAME HENS	1-2 (PER HEN)

FOUR FAST, EASY WAYS TO SHRED CHICKEN

- After cooking boneless skinless chicken breasts in the electric pressure cooker, use a hand mixer right in the pot to quickly shred the meat for recipes.

- Cut cooked chicken into chunks and add it to a stand mixer with the paddle attachment. A few seconds on medium-low speed is just enough to shred it.

- Use 2 large forks to pull cooked chicken in opposite directions.

- After the chicken has cooled a little, pull it into shreds with your hands.

CAJUN-STYLE BEANS & SAUSAGE

Beans and rice make the perfect meal because they're well-balanced, an excellent source of protein and easy to prepare. Sausage adds full flavor to the recipe, and traditional pork sausage lovers won't even notice the switch to chicken sausage.
—Robin Haas, Cranston, RI

Prep: 25 min.
Cook: 5 min. + releasing
Makes: 8 servings

- 1 pkg. (12 oz.) fully cooked spicy chicken sausage links, halved lengthwise and cut into ½-in. slices
- ¾ cup reduced-sodium chicken broth
- 2 cans (16 oz. each) red beans, rinsed and drained
- 2 cans (14½ oz. each) diced tomatoes, undrained
- 3 medium carrots, chopped
- 1 large onion, chopped
- 1 large green pepper, chopped
- ½ cup chopped roasted sweet red peppers
- 3 garlic cloves, minced
- 1 tsp. Cajun seasoning
- 1 tsp. dried oregano
- ½ tsp. dried thyme
- ½ tsp. pepper
- 5⅓ cups cooked brown rice

1. Select saute or browning setting on a 6-qt. electric pressure cooker. Adjust for medium heat; brown sausage. Add broth; cook 1 minute, stirring to loosen browned bits. Press cancel. Stir in beans, tomatoes, vegetables, garlic and seasonings.

2. Lock lid; close pressure-release valve. Adjust to pressure-cook on high for 5 minutes. Let pressure release naturally for 10 minutes; quick-release any remaining pressure. Serve with hot brown rice.

FREEZE OPTION: Freeze cooled meat mixture in freezer containers. To use, partially thaw in refrigerator overnight. Microwave, covered, on high in a microwave-safe dish until heated through, stirring gently and adding a little water if necessary.

1 CUP SAUSAGE AND BEAN MIXTURE WITH ⅔ CUP RICE: 377 cal., 5g fat (1g sat. fat), 33mg chol., 826mg sod., 63g carb. (7g sugars, 10g fiber), 18g pro.

MUSHROOM CHICKEN & PEAS

This meal-in-one recipe was inspired by some amazingly fresh mushrooms I found at our local farmers market. When you start with the best ingredients, you just can't go wrong.
—Jenn Tidwell, Fair Oaks, CA

Prep: 10 min.
Cook: 10 min.
Makes: 4 servings

- 4 boneless skinless chicken breast halves (6 oz. each)
- 1 envelope onion mushroom soup mix
- ½ lb. baby portobello mushrooms, sliced
- 1 medium onion, chopped
- ¾ cup water
- 4 garlic cloves, minced
- 2 cups frozen peas, thawed

1. Place chicken in a 6-qt. electric pressure cooker. Sprinkle with soup mix, pressing to help seasonings adhere. Add mushrooms, onion, water and garlic. Lock lid; close pressure-release valve. Adjust to pressure-cook on high for 6 minutes.

2. Quick-release pressure. Press cancel. A thermometer inserted in chicken should read at least 165°. Select saute setting and adjust for low heat. Add peas; simmer, uncovered, until peas are tender, 3-5 minutes, stirring occasionally.

1 CHICKEN BREAST HALF WITH ¾ CUP VEGETABLE MIXTURE: 282 cal., 5g fat (1g sat. fat), 94mg chol., 558mg sod., 18g carb. (6g sugars, 4g fiber), 41g pro. **DIABETIC EXCHANGES:** 5 lean meat, 1 starch, 1 vegetable.

TEST KITCHEN TIP
Make frozen peas a staple in your home. They're perfect to toss into pasta dishes, salads, soups, stews and casseroles. Best of all, they thaw quickly under warm water, making it a snap to add a bit of color (and nutrition) to your dishes.

HERBED TURKEY BREASTS

Here tender turkey breast is enhanced with an array of flavorful herbs in this juicy, flavorful and comforting dish. What a fabulous way to save time on holiday meals.
—Laurie Mace, Los Osos, CA

Prep: 25 min. + marinating
Cook: 20 min. + releasing
Makes: 12 servings

- 1 can (14½ oz.) chicken broth
- ½ cup lemon juice
- ¼ cup packed brown sugar
- ¼ cup fresh sage
- ¼ cup fresh thyme leaves
- ¼ cup lime juice
- ¼ cup cider vinegar
- ¼ cup olive oil
- 1 envelope onion soup mix
- 2 Tbsp. Dijon mustard
- 1 Tbsp. minced fresh marjoram
- 1½ tsp. paprika
- 1 tsp. garlic powder
- 1 tsp. pepper
- ½ tsp. salt
- 2 boneless skinless turkey breast halves (2 lbs. each) Lemon wedges, optional

1. In a blender, process the first 15 ingredients until blended. Place turkey in a bowl or shallow dish; pour marinade over turkey and turn to coat. Refrigerate, covered, 8 hours or overnight, turning occasionally.

2. Transfer turkey and marinade to a 6-qt. electric pressure cooker. Lock lid; close pressure-release valve. Adjust to pressure-cook on high for 20 minutes.

3. Let pressure release naturally for 10 minutes; quick-release any remaining pressure. A thermometer inserted in turkey breasts should read at least 165°. Remove the turkey from pressure cooker; tent with foil. Let stand 10 minutes before slicing. If desired, top with additional fresh thyme and marjoram and serve with lemon wedges.

5 OZ. COOKED TURKEY: 219 cal., 5g fat (1g sat. fat), 87mg chol., 484mg sod., 5g carb. (3g sugars, 0 fiber), 36g pro. **DIABETIC EXCHANGES:** 5 lean meat.

GARLIC CHICKEN & BROCCOLI

This simple riff on a classic Chinese chicken dish proves you can savor the takeout taste you crave while still eating right.
—Connie Krupp, Racine, WI

Prep: 15 min.
Cook: 5 min.
Makes: 8 servings

- 2 lbs. boneless skinless chicken breasts, cut into 1-in. pieces
- 4 cups fresh broccoli florets
- 4 medium carrots, julienned
- 1 can (8 oz.) sliced water chestnuts, drained
- 6 garlic cloves, minced
- 3 cups reduced-sodium chicken broth
- ¼ cup reduced-sodium soy sauce
- 2 Tbsp. brown sugar
- 2 Tbsp. sesame oil
- 2 Tbsp. rice vinegar
- ½ tsp. salt
- ½ tsp. pepper
- ⅓ cup cornstarch
- ⅓ cup water
  Hot cooked rice

1. Place the first 5 ingredients in a 6-qt. electric pressure cooker. In a large bowl, mix broth, soy sauce, brown sugar, sesame oil, vinegar, salt and pepper; pour over chicken mixture. Lock lid; close pressure-release valve. Adjust to pressure-cook on high for 3 minutes. Quick-release pressure. Press cancel. A thermometer inserted in chicken should read at least 165°.

2. Remove chicken and vegetables; keep warm. In a small bowl, mix cornstarch and water until smooth; stir into cooking juices. Select saute setting and adjust for low heat. Simmer, stirring constantly, until thickened, 1-2 minutes. Serve with chicken, vegetables and hot cooked rice.

FREEZE OPTION: Place chicken and vegetables in freezer containers; top with sauce. Cool and freeze. To use, partially thaw in refrigerator overnight. Microwave, covered, on high in a microwave-safe dish until heated through, stirring gently and adding a little broth or water if necessary.

1 CUP: 241 cal., 6g fat (1g sat. fat), 63mg chol., 798mg sod., 19g carb. (8g sugars, 3g fiber), 26g pro. **DIABETIC EXCHANGES:** 3 lean meat, 1 vegetable, ½ starch, ½ fat.

AUTUMN APPLE CHICKEN

Chicken with apples and barbecue sauce fills the whole house with the most delicious aroma! This is a meal you won't want to wait to dig into.
—Caitlyn Hauser, Brookline, NH

Prep: 25 min.
Cook: 20 min. + releasing
Makes: 4 servings

- 4 bone-in chicken thighs (about 1½ lbs.), skin removed
- ¼ tsp. salt
- ¼ tsp. pepper
- 1 Tbsp. canola oil
- ½ cup apple cider or juice
- 1 medium onion, chopped
- ⅓ cup barbecue sauce
- 1 Tbsp. honey
- 1 garlic clove, minced
- 2 medium Fuji or Gala apples, coarsely chopped

1. Sprinkle chicken with salt and pepper. Select saute or browning setting on a 6-qt. electric pressure cooker. Adjust for medium heat; add oil. When oil is hot, brown chicken; remove and keep warm.

2. Add apple cider, stirring to loosen browned bits from pan. Stir in the onion, barbecue sauce, honey, garlic and chicken. Press cancel. Lock lid; close pressure-release valve. Adjust to pressure-cook on high for 10 minutes. Let pressure release naturally for 5 minutes; quick-release any remaining pressure. Press cancel. A thermometer inserted in chicken should read at least 170°.

3. Remove chicken; keep warm. Select saute setting and adjust for low heat. Add apples; simmer, stirring constantly, until apples are tender, about 10 minutes. Serve with chicken.

1 CHICKEN THIGH WITH ½ CUP APPLE MIXTURE: 340 cal., 13g fat (3g sat. fat), 87mg chol., 458mg sod., 31g carb. (24g sugars, 3g fiber), 25g pro. **DIABETIC EXCHANGES:** 4 lean meat, 1½ starch, ½ fruit.

CHICKEN WITH RAISINS & CAPERS

Capers, golden raisins and fresh basil give this dish a sweetly savory flavor.
And what's even better than that? The kids love it!
—Nadine Mesch, Mount Healthy, OH

Prep: 25 min.
Cook: 10 min.
Makes: 8 servings

- 2 **Tbsp. olive oil, divided**
- 8 **boneless skinless chicken thighs (4 oz. each)**
- 1 **tsp. salt**
- 1 **tsp. pepper**
- ½ **cup Marsala wine**
- ½ **lb. sliced fresh mushrooms**
- 1 **medium sweet red pepper, thinly sliced**
- 1 **medium onion, thinly sliced**
- 1 **can (14½ oz.) diced tomatoes, undrained**
- ½ **cup golden raisins**
- 2 **Tbsp. capers, drained**
- ¼ **cup chopped fresh basil Hot cooked couscous**

1. Select saute or browning setting on a 6-qt. electric pressure cooker. Adjust for medium heat; add 1 Tbsp. oil. Sprinkle the chicken with salt and pepper. When oil is hot, brown chicken in batches. Add wine to pressure cooker. Cook 1 minute and stir to loosen browned bits from pan. Press cancel. Return chicken to pressure cooker.

2. Stir mushrooms, red pepper, onion, and tomatoes, raisins and capers into pressure cooker. Lock lid; close pressure-release valve. Adjust to pressure-cook on high for 6 minutes. Quick-release pressure. A thermometer inserted in chicken should read at least 170°. Sprinkle with basil before serving. Serve with hot cooked couscous.

FREEZE OPTION: Place chicken and vegetables in freezer containers; top with cooking juices. Cool and freeze. To use, partially thaw in refrigerator overnight. Heat through in a covered saucepan, stirring gently and adding a little water if necessary.

1 SERVING: 250 cal., 12g fat (3g sat. fat), 76mg chol., 494mg sod., 13g carb. (9g sugars, 2g fiber), 23g pro. **DIABETIC EXCHANGES:** 3 lean meat, 1 starch, 1 fat.

INDIAN-STYLE CHICKEN & VEGETABLES

This easy Indian-influenced dish is one just about everyone will love. Feel free to add more or less tikka masala sauce according to your taste.
—Erica Polly, Sun Prairie, WI

Prep: 15 min.
Cook: 5 min.
Makes: 8 servings

- 2 **lbs. boneless skinless chicken thighs, cubed**
- 2 **medium sweet potatoes, peeled and cut into 1½-in. pieces**
- 2 **medium sweet red peppers, cut into 1-in. pieces**
- 3 **cups fresh cauliflowerets**
- 2 **jars (15 oz. each) tikka masala curry sauce**
- ½ **cup water**
- ¾ **tsp. salt**
  Minced fresh cilantro, optional
  Naan flatbreads, warmed

In a 6-qt. electric pressure cooker, combine the chicken and vegetables; add sauce, water and salt. Lock lid; close pressure-release valve. Adjust to pressure-cook on high for 3 minutes. Quick-release pressure. A thermometer inserted in chicken should read at least 170°. If desired, top with cilantro; serve with warmed naan.

FREEZE OPTION: Omitting cilantro and naan, freeze cooled chicken and vegetable mixture in freezer containers. To use, partially thaw in refrigerator overnight. Microwave, covered, on high in a microwave-safe dish until heated through, stirring gently and adding a little water if necessary. If desired, sprinkle with cilantro. Serve with warmed naan.

1¼ **CUPS:** 334 cal., 15g fat (4g sat. fat), 80mg chol., 686mg sod., 25g carb. (12g sugars, 5g fiber), 25g pro. **DIABETIC EXCHANGES:** 3 lean meat, 2 fat, 1½ starch.

TEST KITCHEN TIP
Tikka masala is a reddish orange sauce sometimes used in Indian dishes. The spicy ingredient can be found in the ethnic foods aisle of larger grocery stores.

ITALIAN TURKEY BREAST

This recipe makes some of the most succulent turkey I've ever eaten. High in lean protein, it's a smart entree for special occasions.
—Jessica Kunz, Springfield, IL

Prep: 25 min. + standing
Cook: 25 min. + releasing
Makes: 14 servings

- 1 lb. carrots, cut into 2-in. pieces
- 2 medium onions, cut into wedges
- 3 celery ribs, cut into 2-in. pieces
- 1 can (14½ oz.) chicken broth
- 1 bone-in turkey breast (6 to 7 lbs.), thawed and skin removed
- 2 Tbsp. olive oil
- 1½ tsp. seasoned salt
- 1 tsp. Italian seasoning
- ½ tsp. pepper

1. Place vegetables and broth in a 6-qt. electric pressure cooker. Brush turkey with oil; sprinkle with seasonings. Place over vegetables.

2. Lock lid; close pressure-release valve. Adjust to pressure-cook on high for 25 minutes. Let pressure release naturally for 10 minutes; quick-release any remaining pressure. A thermometer inserted in turkey breast should read at least 170°. Remove turkey from pressure cooker; tent with foil. Let stand 10 minutes before slicing.

1 SERVING: 308 cal., 13g fat (3g sat. fat), 106mg chol., 409mg sod., 5g carb. (2g sugars, 1g fiber), 41g pro. **DIABETIC EXCHANGES:** 5 lean meat, ½ fat.

SPICY LIME CHICKEN

This tender chicken with a light lime flavor is ideal as a taco filling, but my son also loves it spooned over cooked rice and finished off with his favorite taco toppings.
—Christine Hair, Odessa, FL

Prep: 10 min.
Cook: 10 min.
Makes: 6 servings

- 4 **boneless skinless chicken breast halves (6 oz. each)**
- 2 **cups chicken broth**
- 3 **Tbsp. lime juice**
- 1 **Tbsp. chili powder**
- 1 **tsp. grated lime zest Fresh cilantro leaves, optional**

DID YOU KNOW?
You can make your own chili powder. Just combine ¼ cup paprika with 1 Tbsp. each garlic powder, onion powder and dried oregano. Stir in 2 tsp. cumin.

1. Place chicken in a 6-qt. electric pressure cooker. Combine broth, lime juice and chili powder; pour over chicken. Lock lid; close pressure-release valve. Adjust to pressure-cook on high for 6 minutes.

2. Quick-release pressure. A thermometer inserted in chicken should read at least 165°.

3. Remove the chicken. When cool enough to handle, shred meat with 2 forks; return to pressure cooker. Stir in lime zest. If desired, serve with cilantro.

FREEZE OPTION: Freeze cooled meat mixture in freezer containers. To use, partially thaw in refrigerator overnight. Microwave, covered, on high in a microwave-safe dish until heated through, stirring gently and adding a little broth if necessary.

1 SERVING: 132 cal., 3g fat (1g sat. fat), 64mg chol., 420mg sod., 2g carb. (1g sugars, 1g fiber), 23g pro. **DIABETIC EXCHANGES:** 3 lean meat.

SPRING-THYME CHICKEN STEW

During a particularly long winter, we were in need of something warm and bright. This stew always reminds me of the days Mom made her chicken soup for me.
—Amy Chase, Vanderhoof, BC

Prep: 25 min.
Cook: 10 min.
Makes: 4 servings

- 1 **lb. small red potatoes, halved**
- 1 **large onion, finely chopped**
- ¾ **cup shredded carrots**
- 6 **garlic cloves, minced**
- 2 **tsp. grated lemon zest**
- 2 **tsp. dried thyme**
- ½ **tsp. salt**
- ¼ **tsp. pepper**
- 1½ **lbs. boneless skinless chicken thighs, cut into 1-in. pieces**
- 2 **cups reduced-sodium chicken broth, divided**
- 2 **bay leaves**
- 3 **Tbsp. all-purpose flour**
- 2 **Tbsp. minced fresh parsley**

1. Place potatoes, onion and carrots in a 6-qt. electric pressure cooker. Top with garlic, lemon zest, thyme, salt and pepper. Place chicken over top. Add 1¾ cups broth and bay leaves.

2. Lock lid; close pressure-release valve. Adjust to pressure-cook on high for 5 minutes. Quick-release pressure. Press cancel. A thermometer inserted in chicken should read at least 170°.

3. Remove chicken; keep warm. Discard bay leaves. In a small bowl, mix flour and remaining ¼ cup broth until smooth; stir into pressure cooker. Select saute setting and adjust for low heat. Simmer, stirring constantly, until slightly thickened, for 1-2 minutes. Return chicken to pressure cooker; heat through. Sprinkle servings with parsley.

1 SERVING: 389 cal., 13g fat (3g sat. fat), 113mg chol., 699mg sod., 31g carb. (4g sugars, 4g fiber), 37g pro. **DIABETIC EXCHANGES:** 5 lean meat, 2 vegetable, 1½ starch.

SAUCY BARBECUE CHICKEN THIGHS

Barbecued chicken gets a makeover in this recipe. The combination of ingredients makes for a mellow, not-too-sweet flavor that's more grown-up than the original and super over rice, pasta or potatoes.
—Sharon Fritz, Morristown, TN

Prep: 15 min.
Cook: 10 min.
Makes: 6 servings

- 6 **boneless skinless chicken thighs (about 1½ lbs.)**
- ½ tsp. **poultry seasoning**
- 1 **medium onion, chopped**
- 1 **can (14½ oz.) diced tomatoes, undrained**
- 1 **can (8 oz.) tomato sauce**
- ½ cup **barbecue sauce**
- ¼ cup **water**
- ¼ cup **orange juice**
- 1 tsp. **garlic powder**
- ¾ tsp. **dried oregano**
- ½ tsp. **hot pepper sauce**
- ¼ tsp. **pepper**
  Hot cooked brown rice, optional

1. Place chicken in a 6-qt. electric pressure cooker; sprinkle with poultry seasoning. Top with onion and tomatoes. In a small bowl, mix the tomato sauce, barbecue sauce, water, orange juice and seasonings; pour over top.

2. Lock lid; close pressure-release valve. Adjust to pressure-cook on high for 10 minutes. Quick-release pressure. A thermometer inserted in chicken should read at least 170° If desired, serve with rice.

FREEZE OPTION: Place cooked chicken mixture in freezer containers. Cool and freeze. To use, partially thaw in refrigerator overnight. Microwave, covered, on high in a microwave-safe dish until heated through, gently stirring and adding a little water if necessary.

1 SERVING: 240 cal., 9g fat (2g sat. fat), 76mg chol., 582mg sod., 18g carb. (12g sugars, 2g fiber), 23g pro. **DIABETIC EXCHANGES:** 3 lean meat, 1 starch.

WHY YOU'LL LOVE IT...

"This was surprisingly good, especially considering how easy the prep is. Definitely recommend serving over rice. Lots of sauce. Very yummy."
—CHRIS, TASTEOFHOME.COM

LEMON CHICKEN WITH BASIL

No matter when I eat it, this tangy chicken dish always reminds me of summer meals with friends and family. The recipe produces a lot of lovely sauce; serve it as is or spoon it over some lightly herbed couscous.
—Deborah Posey, VA Beach, VA

Prep: 10 min.
Cook: 10 min.
Makes: 4 servings

- 4 **boneless skinless chicken breast halves (6 oz. each)**
- 2 **medium lemons**
- 1 **bunch fresh basil leaves (¾ oz.)**
- 2 **cups chicken stock**

TEST KITCHEN TIP
Lemon zest is the outer peel or rind. To remove the zest, peel thin strips with a small sharp knife, being careful not to include the white bitter membrane, and mince finely. You can also take the whole fruit and rub it over a hand grater.

1. Place the chicken in a 6-qt. electric pressure cooker. Finely grate enough zest from lemons to measure 4 tsp. Cut lemons in half; squeeze juice. Add zest and juice to pressure cooker.

2. Tear fresh basil leaves directly into pressure cooker; add chicken stock. Lock lid; close pressure-release valve. Adjust to pressure-cook on high for 6 minutes. Quick-release pressure. A thermometer inserted in chicken should read at least 165°. When cool enough to handle, shred meat with 2 forks; return to pressure cooker. If desired, stir in additional lemon zest and chopped basil. Serve with a slotted spoon.

FREEZE OPTION: Place chicken and cooking liquid in freezer containers. Cool and freeze. To use, partially thaw in the refrigerator overnight. Microwave, covered, on high in a microwave-safe dish until heated through, stirring gently.

5 OZ. COOKED CHICKEN: 200 cal., 4g fat (1g sat. fat), 94mg chol., 337mg sod., 3g carb. (1g sugars, 0 fiber), 37g pro. **DIABETIC EXCHANGES:** 5 lean meat.

ORANGE CHIPOTLE CHICKEN

The citrus in this delicious chicken entree keeps things fresh and lively. We're big on spice in our house, so sometimes I use two chipotle peppers.
—Deborah Biggs, Omaha, NE

Prep: 15 min.
Cook: 10 min.
Makes: 6 servings

½ cup plus 2 Tbsp. cold water, divided
½ cup thawed orange juice concentrate
¼ cup barbecue sauce
1 chipotle pepper in adobo sauce
¼ tsp. salt
¼ tsp. garlic powder
6 boneless skinless chicken breast halves (6 oz. each)
¼ cup chopped red onion
4 tsp. cornstarch
Grated orange zest

1. Place ½ cup water, orange juice concentrate, barbecue sauce, chipotle pepper, salt and garlic powder in a blender; cover and process until blended.

2. Place chicken and onion in a 6-qt. electric pressure cooker; top with juice mixture. Lock lid; close pressure-release valve. Adjust to pressure-cook on high for 6 minutes.

3. Quick release pressure. Press cancel. A thermometer inserted in chicken should read at least 165°. Remove the chicken from pressure cooker; keep warm.

4. In a small bowl, mix cornstarch and remaining 2 Tbsp. water until smooth; gradually stir into pressure cooker. Select the saute setting and adjust for low heat. Simmer, stirring constantly, until thickened, 1-2 minutes. Spoon over chicken; top with orange zest.

FREEZE OPTION: Place chicken in freezer containers; top with sauce. Cool and freeze. To use, partially thaw in refrigerator overnight. Heat through in a covered saucepan, stirring gently and adding a little water if necessary.

1 CHICKEN BREAST WITH ¼ CUP SAUCE: 246 cal., 4g fat (1g sat. fat), 94mg chol., 315mg sod., 15g carb. (11g sugars, 1g fiber), 35g pro. **DIABETIC EXCHANGES:** 5 lean meat, 1 starch.

RED PEPPER CHICKEN

Chicken breasts are treated to black beans, red peppers and juicy tomatoes in this southwestern supper. We love it served with rice cooked in chicken broth—and it would also make a fun filling for tacos or burritos.
—Piper Spiwak, Vienna, VA

Prep: 15 min.
Cook: 15 min.
Makes: 4 servings

- 4 **boneless skinless chicken breast halves (4 oz. each)**
- 1 **can (15 oz.) no-salt-added black beans, rinsed and drained**
- 1 **can (14½ oz.) Mexican stewed tomatoes, undrained**
- 1 **jar (12 oz.) roasted sweet red peppers, drained and cut into strips**
- 1 **large onion, chopped**
- ½ **cup water**
  Pepper to taste
  Hot cooked rice

1. Place chicken in a 6-qt. electric pressure cooker. In a bowl, combine beans, tomatoes, red peppers, onion, water and pepper; pour over chicken. Lock lid; close pressure-release valve. Adjust to pressure-cook on high for 5 minutes.

2. Quick-release pressure. Press cancel. A thermometer inserted in chicken should read at least 165°. Remove the chicken and keep warm. Select saute setting; adjust for low heat. Simmer cooking juices until thickened, 8-10 minutes. Serve with rice and chicken.

FREEZE OPTION: Place chicken and bean mixture in freezer containers; top with cooking juices. Cool and freeze. To use, partially thaw in refrigerator overnight. Microwave, covered, on high in a microwave-safe dish until heated through, stirring gently and adding a little broth or water if necessary.

1 CHICKEN BREAST HALF WITH 1 CUP BEAN MIXTURE: 288 cal., 3g fat (1g sat. fat), 63mg chol., 657mg sod., 28g carb. (8g sugars, 7g fiber), 30g pro. **DIABETIC EXCHANGES:** 3 lean meat, 1½ starch, 1 vegetable.

COUNTRY CAPTAIN CHICKEN

Whether it was brought by a British sailor or not, the recipe for Country Captain Chicken has been around Georgia since the 1800s. Traditionally served over rice, it's also delicious with noodles or mashed potatoes.
—Suzanne Banfield, Basking Ridge, NJ

Prep: 25 min.
Cook: 10 min.
Makes: 8 servings

- 1 large onion, chopped
- 1 medium sweet red pepper, chopped
- 2 garlic cloves, minced
- 3 lbs. boneless skinless chicken thighs
- ½ cup chicken broth
- 1 Tbsp. brown sugar
- 1 Tbsp. curry powder
- 1 tsp. ground ginger
- 1 tsp. ground cinnamon
- 1 tsp. dried thyme
- 1 can (14½ oz.) diced tomatoes, undrained
- ½ cup golden raisins or raisins
  Hot cooked rice
  Chopped fresh parsley, optional

1. Place onion, red pepper and garlic in a 6-qt. electric pressure cooker; top with chicken. In a small bowl, whisk broth, brown sugar and seasonings; pour over chicken. Top with tomatoes and raisins. Lock lid; close pressure-release valve. Adjust to pressure-cook on high for 6 minutes.

2. Quick-release pressure. A thermometer inserted in chicken should read at least 170°. Thicken cooking juices if desired. Serve with rice and if desired, parsley.

FREEZE OPTION: Place chicken and vegetables in freezer containers; top with cooking juices. Cool and freeze. To use, partially thaw in refrigerator overnight. Heat through in a covered saucepan, stirring gently and adding a little broth if necessary.

1 SERVING: 298 cal., 13g fat (3g sat. fat), 114mg chol., 159mg sod., 13g carb. (9g sugars, 2g fiber), 32g pro. **DIABETIC EXCHANGES:** 4 lean meat, 1 vegetable, ½ starch.

CHICKEN CHOP SUEY

If you're in for a busy evening, here's a wonderful way to ensure you can still have a healthful supper. It's tasty, traditional—and quick, too.
—Melody Littlewood, Royal City, WA

Prep: 20 min.
Cook: 5 min.
Makes: 9 servings

1½ lbs. boneless skinless chicken thighs, cut into 2-in. pieces
½ lb. sliced fresh mushrooms
2 celery ribs, sliced
1 medium onion, chopped
1 can (14 oz.) bean sprouts, rinsed and drained
1 can (8 oz.) bamboo shoots, drained
1 can (8 oz.) sliced water chestnuts, drained
½ cup frozen shelled edamame
1 can (14½ oz.) reduced-sodium chicken broth
½ cup reduced-sodium soy sauce
1 Tbsp. minced fresh gingerroot
¼ tsp. crushed red pepper flakes
¼ cup cornstarch
¼ cup cold water
Hot cooked rice

1. Place chicken in a 6-qt. electric pressure cooker. Top with mushrooms, celery, onion, bean sprouts, bamboo shoots, water chestnuts and edamame. In a small bowl, combine the broth, soy sauce, ginger and pepper flakes. Pour over chicken and vegetables.

2. Lock lid; close pressure-release valve. Adjust to pressure-cook on high for 3 minutes. Quick-release pressure. Press cancel. A thermometer inserted in chicken should read at least 170°.

3. Select saute setting and adjust for low heat. In a small bowl, mix cornstarch and water until smooth; stir into the chicken mixture. Simmer, stirring constantly, until thickened, 1-2 minutes. Serve with rice.

1 CUP: 182 cal., 6g fat (2g sat. fat), 50mg chol., 709mg sod., 13g carb. (3g sugars, 2g fiber), 19g pro. **DIABETIC EXCHANGES:** 2 lean meat, 1 vegetable, ½ starch.

DID YOU KNOW?
Edamame come from the soybean that is harvested early, before the beans become hard. The young beans are parboiled and frozen to retain their freshness and can be found in the freezer section of grocery stores.

GENERAL TSO'S STEW

I love Asian food and wanted a chili-style soup with flavors of General Tso. You can use any meat you like—I used leftover pork, but it's great with turkey, chicken or ground meats.
—Lori McLain, Denton, TX

Prep: 10 min.
Cook: 10 min.
Makes: 6 servings

- 1 cup tomato juice
- ½ cup water
- ½ cup pickled cherry peppers, chopped
- 2 Tbsp. soy sauce
- 2 Tbsp. hoisin sauce
- 1 Tbsp. peanut oil
- 1 to 2 tsp. crushed red pepper flakes
- 1 lb. boneless skinless chicken breast halves
- 1½ cups chopped onion
- 1 cup chopped fresh broccoli
- ¼ cup chopped green onions
- 1 tsp. sesame seeds, toasted

1. In a 6-qt. electric pressure cooker, combine the first 7 ingredients. Top with chicken, onion and broccoli. Lock lid; close pressure-release valve. Adjust to pressure-cook on high for 6 minutes. Quick-release pressure. Press cancel. A thermometer inserted in chicken should read at least 165°.

2. Remove chicken; shred with 2 forks. Return to pressure cooker; heat through. Top with green onions and sesame seeds to serve.

FREEZE OPTION: Freeze cooled stew in freezer containers. To use, partially thaw in refrigerator overnight. Heat through in a saucepan, stirring occasionally and adding a little water if necessary.

1 CUP: 159 cal., 5g fat (1g sat. fat), 42mg chol., 762mg sod., 10g carb. (5g sugars, 2g fiber), 18g pro. **DIABETIC EXCHANGES:** 2 lean meat, 2 vegetable, ½ fat.

BEEF ENTREES

Hearty…satisfying…comforting…those are
just a few of the ways to describe the following
stick-to-your-ribs meals. After all, eating healthy
doesn't have to mean cutting out red meat,
so dig in and enjoy tonight!

BEEF 101

It's true! You can trim down meals and continue to enjoy meaty entrees. Follow these tips to learn how.

WHEN BUYING BEEF, LOOK FOR:

- Bright cherry red color in cuts and ground beef. Avoid meat with gray or brown patches.

- Packages free of holes, tears or excessive liquid, which may indicate improper handling and storage.

- Creamy pink color and fine-grain texture in veal. Avoid discolored or dried-out meat.

- A sell-by date on the package that is later than the day of your purchase. If it's the same date, use the meat that day or freeze it for later.

GENERAL GUIDELINES FOR PURCHASE WEIGHT AND SERVINGS

- 1 lb. bone-in roast = roughly 2½ servings

- 1 lb. boneless cut with some fat to be trimmed = about 2½-3½ servings

- 1 lb. lean boneless cut (such as eye of round, flank steak or tenderloin) = 3-4 servings

- 1 lb. bone-in steak = 2 servings

BUYING AND COOKING GROUND BEEF

Ground beef comes from a combination of beef cuts. It is often labeled with the cut of meat that it is ground from, such as ground chuck or ground round. Ground beef also can be labeled according to the fat content of the ground mixture or the percentage of lean meat to fat, such as 85% or 90% lean. The higher the percentage, the leaner the meat. When buying and cooking ground beef:

- Purchase only the amount you need; 1 lb. of ground beef serves 3-4.

- Select ground beef that is bright red in color and is in a tightly sealed package. Purchase ground beef before the sell-by date.

- Handle the mixture as little as possible when shaping hamburgers, meat loaves or meatballs to keep the final product light in texture.

- Cook ground beef until it is well-done and no longer pink. For patties and loaves, where it is difficult to judge color, make sure a thermometer reads 160° before serving.

DEFROSTING GUIDELINES

The thicker the package, the longer it will take to defrost. Here are some guidelines for defrosting beef or veal in the refrigerator:

- For ½ to ¾-in.-thick ground beef or veal patties, allow at least 12 hours.

- For a large roast or a thick pot roast, allow about 6 hours per pound.

- For steaks, allow 12-24 hours.

- For 1 to 1½-in.-thick meat cuts or packages of ground beef or veal, allow at least 24 hours.

RUBS

A rub is a blend of dry seasonings, such as fresh or dried herbs and spices, that coats the surface of uncooked meat to add flavor. Rubs add a lot of flavor without fat, but they do not tenderize meats.

MARINADES

A marinade is mixture of liquid and seasonings used to coat meat before cooking. Marinades both flavor and tenderize meats, but may add more calories, fat and sodium than rubs.

- To truly tenderize meat, a marinade needs an acidic ingredient like lemon juice, vinegar, yogurt or even wine. For the best results, coat the meat completely in the marinade.

- Allow from 6-24 hours to tenderize cuts such as large steaks or roasts. Smaller cuts like cubes or thin steaks can be marinated for a few hours. Used for more than 24 hours, a tenderizing marinade can make the meat mushy.

- Marinate meat at room temperature for no longer than 30 minutes. For longer times marinate meat in the refrigerator.

BEEF UP YOUR MENUS

You'll save time in the kitchen—in addition to calories, fat, sodium and carbohydrates—when you follow these no-fuss menus. Pick an entree below, then simply plan on the side dishes that go with them.

BEEF RECIPE
Beef Burritos with
Green Chiles, Page 176

MENU ADD-ONS
• Avocado slices
• Roasted corn

BEEF RECIPE
Burgundy Beef,
Page 179

MENU ADD-ONS
• Steamed green beans
• Wedge salad

BEEF RECIPE
Spicy Vegetable Stew,
Page 180

MENU ADD-ONS
• Whole wheat bread
• Sugar-free iced tea

BEEF RECIPE
Coffee Beef Roast,
Page 183

MENU ADD-ONS
• Roasted carrots
• Cooked noodles

BEEF RECIPE
Shredded Beef Lettuce
Cups, Page 184

MENU ADD-ONS
• Cucumber slices
• Tomato wedges

BEEF RECIPE
Spice-Braised Pot Roast,
Page 187

MENU ADD-ONS
• Roasted broccoli
• Bran muffins

BEEF RECIPE
Beef Daube Provencal,
Page 188

MENU ADD-ONS
• Sauteed asparagus
• Fat-free vanilla pudding

BEEF RECIPE
Mushroom Pot Roast,
Page 191

MENU ADD-ONS
• Corn
• Angel food cake

BEEF RECIPE
Beef Roast with Asian Black
Bean Sauce, Page 192

MENU ADD-ONS
• Steamed edamame
• Fortune cookies

BEEF RECIPE
Beef & Rice Cabbage Rolls,
Page 195

MENU ADD-ONS
• Cooked rice
• Roasted cauliflower

BEEF RECIPE
Caribbean Pot Roast,
Page 196

MENU ADD-ONS
• Pita bread
• Steamed okra

BEEF RECIPE
Beefy Cabbage & Bean
Stew, Page 199

MENU ADD-ONS
• 7-grain bread
• Spinach salad

BEEF CUTS

Don't be overwhelmed by the many cuts of beef available today. Simply check here before visiting the butcher.

► TENDER   ► LESS TENDER

CHUCK | **RIB** | **SHORT LOIN** | **SIRLOIN** | **ROUND**
BRISKET | **SHANK** | **PLATE** | **FLANK**

► **CHUCK**
CHUCK ARM
POT ROAST

► **CHUCK**
CHUCK SHOULDER
POT ROAST,
BONELESS

▼ **CHUCK**
CHUCK SHOULDER
STEAK, BONELESS

▲ **CHUCK**
COUNTRY-STYLE
RIBS

▼ **CHUCK**
CHUCK 7-BONE
POT ROAST

◄ **RIB**
RIBEYE
ROAST

► **RIB**
RIBEYE
STEAK

► **RIB**
BACK
RIBS

► **CHUCK**
CHUCK MOCK
TENDER
STEAK

▼ **CHUCK**
CHUCK SHORT
RIBS

▼ **RIB**
SHORT
RIBS

► **CHUCK**
CHUCK POT
ROAST,
BONELESS

► **RIB**
RIB ROAST,
LARGE END

◄ **SIRLOIN**
TOP SIRLOIN
STEAK,
BONELESS

▶ **SHORT LOIN**
TOP LOIN
(STRIP) STEAKS

◀ **ROUND**
ROUND
STEAK,
BONELESS

◀ **FLANK**
FLANK
STEAK

▼ **FLANK**
FLANK STEAK,
TRIMMED

▶ **ROUND**
EYE ROUND
ROAST

▶ **SHORT LOIN**
T-BONE
STEAK

◀ **ROUND**
ROUND TIP
ROAST,
CAP OFF

▼ **OTHER CUTS**
GROUND BEEF

▲ **SHORT LOIN**
PORTERHOUSE
STEAK

▶ **BRISKET**
BRISKET,
WHOLE,
BONELESS

▼ **OTHER CUTS**
CUBE STEAKS

▲ **SHORT LOIN**
TENDERLOIN

▼ **OTHER CUTS**
BEEF STRIPS

▼ **SHORT LOIN**
TENDERLOIN ROAST

◀ **BRISKET**
BRISKET,
POINT HALF

▼ **PLATE**
HANGER
STEAK

◀ **OTHER CUTS**
BEEF STEW
MEAT

▶ **SIRLOIN**
BOTTOM
SIRLOIN,
TRI-TIP
ROAST

▼ **PLATE**
INSIDE SKIRT
STEAK

▶ **OTHER CUTS**
KABOB
MEAT

▼ **OTHER CUTS**
SPECIAL TRIM

▲ **ROUND**
TOP ROUND STEAK

▲ **PLATE**
OUTSIDE
SKIRT STEAK

BEEF BURRITOS WITH GREEN CHILES

Here's a family favorite that gets mouths watering simply with its heavenly aroma! Hearty and flavorful, it's quick comfort food.
—Sally J. Pahler, Palisade, CO

Prep: 20 min.
Cook: 1 hour 20 min. + releasing
Makes: 14 servings

- 4 **cans (7 oz. each) whole green chiles, undrained**
- 1 **can (28 oz.) diced tomatoes, undrained**
- 1 **large onion, diced**
- 1 **boneless beef chuck roast (4 lbs.)**
- 2 **garlic cloves, minced**
- 1 **tsp. salt**
- 2 **tsp. ground cumin**
- 1 **tsp. cayenne pepper**
- 14 **whole wheat tortillas (8 in.), warmed**
  Optional toppings:
  Shredded cheddar cheese, salsa, sour cream, sliced ripe olives

1. Drain chiles, reserving liquid. Coarsely chop chiles; place in a 6-qt. electric pressure cooker. Add the tomatoes, onion and reserved drained liquid. Cut roast in half. Combine the garlic, salt, cumin and cayenne; rub over the roast. Place in pressure cooker. Lock the lid; close pressure-release valve. Adjust to pressure-cook on high for 80 minutes. Let pressure release naturally for 10 minutes; quick-release any remaining pressure. A thermometer inserted in the beef should read at least 165°.

2. Remove the roast; shred with 2 forks. Return to pressure cooker; heat through. Using a slotted spoon, serve in tortillas, with toppings if desired.

FREEZE OPTION: Freeze the cooled meat mixture and juices in freezer containers. To use, partially thaw in refrigerator overnight. Heat through in a saucepan, stirring occasionally and adding a little water if necessary.

1 BURRITO: 355 cal., 13g fat (5g sat. fat), 84mg chol., 499mg sod., 28g carb. (4g sugars, 4g fiber), 30g pro. **DIABETIC EXCHANGES:** 4 lean meat, 2 starch, ½ fat.

BURGUNDY BEEF

When my adult children come for dinner, this is the recipe I turn to first. They all just love it!
—Urilla Cheverie, Andover, MA

Prep: 10 min.
Cook: 25 min. + releasing
Makes: 10 servings

4 lbs. beef top
   sirloin steak, cut
   into 1-in. cubes
3 large onions, sliced
1 cup water
1 cup burgundy wine
   or beef broth
1 cup ketchup
¼ cup quick-cooking
   tapioca
¼ cup packed
   brown sugar
¼ cup Worcestershire
   sauce
4 tsp. paprika
1½ tsp. salt
1 tsp. minced garlic
1 tsp. ground mustard
2 Tbsp. cornstarch
3 Tbsp. cold water
   Hot cooked noodles

1. Combine the first 12 ingredients in a 6-qt. electric pressure cooker. Lock lid; close pressure-release valve. Adjust to pressure-cook on high for 20 minutes. Let pressure release naturally for 10 minutes; quick-release any remaining pressure. Press cancel.

2. Combine cornstarch and cold water until smooth; stir into pressure cooker. Select saute setting and adjust for low heat. Simmer, stirring constantly, until thickened, 1-2 minutes. Serve with noodles.

FREEZE OPTION: Place beef in freezer containers; top with sauce. Cool and freeze. To use, partially thaw in refrigerator overnight. Heat through in a covered saucepan, stirring gently and adding a little water if necessary.

1 CUP: 347 cal., 8g fat (3g sat. fat), 74mg chol., 811mg sod., 24g carb. (15g sugars, 1g fiber), 40g pro.

SPICY BEEF VEGETABLE STEW

This zesty ground beef and vegetable soup is flavorful and comes together so quickly. It makes a complete meal when served with warm cornbread, sourdough or French bread, if you can squeak in a few more calories.
—Lynnette Davis, Tullahoma, TN

Prep: 10 min.
Cook: 5 min. + releasing
Makes: 8 servings (3 qt.)

- 1 lb. lean ground beef (90% lean)
- 3½ cups water
- 1 jar (24 oz.) meatless pasta sauce
- 1 pkg. (16 oz.) frozen mixed vegetables
- 1 can (10 oz.) diced tomatoes and green chiles, undrained
- 1 cup chopped onion
- 1 cup sliced celery
- 1 tsp. beef bouillon granules
- 1 tsp. pepper

Select saute or browning setting on a 6-qt. electric pressure cooker; adjust for medium heat. Cook beef until no longer pink, 6-8 minutes, breaking into crumbles; drain. Stir in the remaining ingredients. Lock lid; close pressure-release valve. Adjust to pressure-cook on high for 5 minutes. Let pressure release naturally.

FREEZE OPTION: Freeze cooled stew in freezer containers. To use, partially thaw in refrigerator overnight. Heat through in a saucepan, stirring occasionally and adding a little water if necessary.

1½ **CUPS:** 177 cal., 5g fat (2g sat. fat), 35mg chol., 675mg sod., 19g carb. (8g sugars, 5g fiber), 15g pro. **DIABETIC EXCHANGES:** 2 lean meat, 1 starch.

WHY YOU'LL LOVE IT...

"What I loved most about this recipe is everything in it is something I have in my stock of food—there was nothing else I had to go and buy. It is amazing, really good."
—BONITO15, TASTEOFHOME.COM

COFFEE BEEF ROAST

Your morning brew is the key to this flavorful roast that simmers until it's fall-apart tender. Try it once, and I'm sure you'll cook it again.
—Charles Trahan, San Dimas, CA

Prep: 15 min.
Cook: 55 min. + releasing
Makes: 6 servings

2 tsp. canola oil
1 beef sirloin tip roast
   (2½ lbs.), halved
1½ cups brewed coffee
1½ cups sliced fresh
   mushrooms
⅓ cup sliced green onions
2 garlic cloves, minced
1 tsp. liquid smoke,
   optional
½ tsp. salt
½ tsp. chili powder
¼ tsp. pepper
¼ cup cornstarch
⅓ cup cold water

1. Select the saute or browning setting on a 6-qt. electric pressure cooker. Adjust for medium heat; add 1 tsp. oil. When oil is hot, brown a roast half on all sides. Remove; repeat with remaining beef and oil. Add coffee to pressure cooker. Cook 1 minute, stirring to loosen browned bits from the pan. Press cancel. Add mushrooms, green onions, garlic, liquid smoke if desired, salt, chili powder, pepper and beef.

2. Lock lid; close pressure-release valve. Adjust to pressure-cook on high for 50 minutes. Let pressure release naturally. A thermometer inserted in beef should read at least 145°. Press cancel.

3. Remove the roast and vegetables to a serving platter; tent with foil. Let stand 10 minutes before slicing. Reserve 2 cups cooking juices; discard the remaining juices. Transfer back to pressure cooker. In a small bowl, mix cornstarch and water until smooth; stir into pressure cooker. Select saute setting and adjust for low heat. Simmer, stirring constantly, until thickened, 1-2 minutes. Serve with roast and vegetables.

FREEZE OPTION: Place the sliced pot roast and vegetables in freezer containers; top with the sauce. Cool and freeze. To use, partially thaw in the refrigerator overnight. Heat through in a covered saucepan, stirring gently and adding a little water if necessary.

5 OZ. COOKED BEEF: 281 cal., 10g fat (3g sat. fat), 120mg chol., 261mg sod., 6g carb. (1g sugars, 0 fiber), 39g pro. **DIABETIC EXCHANGES:** 5 lean meat, ½ starch.

SHREDDED BEEF LETTUCE CUPS

I love this light yet lively dinner for busy days filled with swim lessons and outdoor activities. If you can't find Bibb or Boston, try green leaf lettuce—it's less sturdy but works in a pinch.
—Elisabeth Larsen, Pleasant Grove, UT

Prep: 20 min.
Cook: 40 min. + releasing
Makes: 8 servings

- 3 medium carrots, chopped
- 2 medium sweet red peppers, chopped
- 1 medium onion, chopped
- 1 boneless beef chuck roast (2 lbs.)
- 1 can (8 oz.) unsweetened crushed pineapple, undrained
- ½ cup reduced-sodium soy sauce
- 2 Tbsp. brown sugar
- 2 Tbsp. white vinegar
- 1 garlic clove, minced
- ½ tsp. pepper
- 3 Tbsp. cornstarch
- 3 Tbsp. water
- 24 Bibb or Boston lettuce leaves
  Sliced green onions, optional

1. Combine carrots, red peppers and onion in a 6-qt. pressure cooker. Top with roast. In a small bowl, combine pineapple, soy sauce, brown sugar, vinegar, garlic and pepper; pour over roast. Lock lid; close pressure-release valve. Adjust to pressure-cook on high for 40 minutes. Let pressure release naturally. Press cancel. Remove roast from pressure cooker. Cool slightly; shred roast with 2 forks.

2. Skim fat from cooking juices; return juices and vegetables to pressure cooker. In a small bowl, mix cornstarch and water until smooth; stir into pressure cooker. Select saute setting and adjust for low heat. Simmer, stirring constantly, until thickened, 1-2 minutes. Return shredded meat to pressure cooker; heat through.

3. Serve in lettuce leaves. If desired, sprinkle with onions.

FREEZE OPTION: Freeze the cooled meat mixture and sauce in freezer containers. To use, partially thaw in refrigerator overnight. Heat through in a saucepan, stirring occasionally and adding a little water if necessary.

3 LETTUCE CUPS: 270 cal., 11g fat (4g sat. fat), 74mg chol., 641mg sod., 17g carb. (10g sugars, 2g fiber), 24g pro. **DIABETIC EXCHANGES:** 3 lean meat, 1 starch.

SPICE-BRAISED POT ROAST

Herbs and spices give this beef an excellent flavor. I often serve the roast over egg noodles or with mashed potatoes, using the juices as a gravy.
—Loren Martin, Big Cabin, OK

Prep: 15 min.
Cook: 50 min. + releasing
Makes: 8 servings

- 1 **boneless beef chuck roast (2½ lbs.), halved**
- 1 **can (14½ oz.) diced tomatoes, undrained**
- 1 **medium onion, chopped**
- ½ **cup water**
- ¼ **cup white vinegar**
- 3 **Tbsp. tomato puree**
- 1 **Tbsp. poppy seeds**
- 1 **bay leaf**
- 2¼ **tsp. sugar**
- 2 **tsp. Dijon mustard**
- 2 **garlic cloves, minced**
- ½ **tsp. salt**
- ½ **tsp. ground ginger**
- ½ **tsp. dried rosemary, crushed**
- ½ **tsp. lemon juice**
- ¼ **tsp. ground cumin**
- ¼ **tsp. ground turmeric**
- ¼ **tsp. crushed red pepper flakes**
- ⅛ **tsp. ground cloves**
  Hot cooked egg noodles

1. Place beef roast in a 6-qt. electric pressure cooker. Mix all remaining ingredients except egg noodles; pour over roast. Lock lid; close pressure-release valve. Adjust to pressure-cook on high for 50 minutes. Let pressure release naturally. A thermometer inserted in beef should read at least 145°.

2. Discard bay leaf. If desired, skim fat and thicken cooking juices. Serve pot roast with noodles and juices.

FREEZE OPTION: Place the pot roast in freezer containers; top with cooking juices. Cool and freeze. To use, partially thaw in refrigerator overnight. Heat through in a covered saucepan, stirring gently and adding a little water if necessary.

1 SERVING: 272 cal., 14g fat (5g sat. fat), 92mg chol., 320mg sod., 6g carb. (4g sugars, 1g fiber), 29g pro. **DIABETIC EXCHANGES:** 4 lean meat, ½ starch.›

TEST KITCHEN TIP
If you can insert a carving fork into the thickest part of the roast easily, it is near done. If it's cooked until it falls apart, the meat is actually overcooked and will be stringy, tough and dry.

BEEF DAUBE PROVENCAL

My dinner is perfect for us on chilly nights, especially after we've been out chopping wood. The melt-in-your-mouth goodness makes it a staple in my menu rotation.
—Brenda Ryan, Marshall, MO

Prep: 30 min.
Cook: 30 min. + releasing
Makes: 8 servings

- 1 boneless beef chuck roast or venison roast (about 2 lbs.), cut into 1-in. cubes
- 1½ tsp. salt, divided
- ½ tsp. coarsely ground pepper, divided
- 2 tsp. olive oil
- 2 cups chopped carrots
- 1½ cups chopped onion
- 12 garlic cloves, crushed
- 1 Tbsp. tomato paste
- 1 cup dry red wine
- 1 can (14½ oz.) diced tomatoes, undrained
- ½ cup beef broth
- 1 tsp. chopped fresh rosemary
- 1 tsp. chopped fresh thyme
- 1 bay leaf
   Dash ground cloves
   Hot cooked pasta or mashed potatoes

1. Sprinkle the beef with ½ tsp. salt and ¼ tsp. pepper. Select saute or browning setting on a 6-qt. electric pressure cooker. Adjust for medium heat; add oil. When oil is hot, brown beef in batches.

2. Add carrots, onions and garlic to pressure cooker; cook and stir until golden brown, 4-6 minutes. Add tomato paste; cook and stir until fragrant, about 1 minute. Add red wine, stirring to loosen browned bits. Return the beef to pressure cooker. Add tomatoes, broth, rosemary, thyme, bay leaf, cloves and remaining 1 tsp. salt and ¼ tsp. pepper. Press cancel.

3. Lock lid; close pressure-release valve. Adjust to pressure-cook on high for 30 minutes. Let pressure release naturally for 10 minutes; quick-release any remaining pressure. A thermometer inserted in the beef should read at least 160°. Discard the bay leaf. Serve with hot cooked pasta. If desired, sprinkle with additional thyme.

FREEZE OPTION: Place the beef and vegetables in freezer containers; top with cooking juices. Cool and freeze. To use, partially thaw in the refrigerator overnight. Heat through in a covered saucepan, stirring gently and adding a little broth if necessary.

1 CUP BEEF MIXTURE: 248 cal., 12g fat (4g sat. fat), 74mg chol., 652mg sod., 10g carb. (5g sugars, 2g fiber), 24g pro. **DIABETIC EXCHANGES:** 3 lean meat, 1 vegetable.

MUSHROOM POT ROAST

Packed with wholesome veggies and tender beef, this is an entree that will delight all ages. Serve mashed potatoes alongside to soak up every last drop of gravy.
—Angie Stewart, Topeka, KS

Prep: 25 min.
Cook: 65 min. + releasing
Makes: 10 servings

- 1 boneless beef chuck roast (3 to 4 lbs.)
- ½ tsp. salt
- ¼ tsp. pepper
- 1 Tbsp. canola oil
- 1½ cups dry red wine or reduced-sodium beef broth
- 1½ lbs. sliced fresh shiitake mushrooms
- 2½ cups thinly sliced onions
- 1½ cups reduced-sodium beef broth
- 1 can (8 oz.) tomato sauce
- ¾ cup chopped peeled parsnips
- ¾ cup chopped celery
- ¾ cup chopped carrots
- 8 garlic cloves, minced
- 2 bay leaves
- 1½ tsp. dried thyme
- 1 tsp. chili powder
- ¼ cup cornstarch
- ¼ cup water
  Mashed potatoes

1. Halve roast; sprinkle with salt and pepper. Select saute or browning setting on a 6-qt. electric pressure cooker. Adjust for medium heat; add 1½ tsp. oil. When oil is hot, brown a roast half on all sides. Remove; repeat with remaining beef and 1½ tsp. oil. Add wine to pressure cooker. Cook 2 minutes, stirring to loosen browned bits from pan. Press cancel. Return beef to pressure cooker.

2. Add mushrooms, onions, broth, tomato sauce, parsnips, celery, carrots, garlic, bay leaves, thyme and chili powder. Lock lid; close pressure-release valve. Adjust to pressure-cook on high for 60 minutes. Let the pressure release naturally for 10 minutes; quick-release any remaining pressure. Press cancel. A thermometer inserted in the beef roast should read at least 160°.

3. Remove meat and vegetables to a serving platter; keep warm. Discard the bay leaves. Skim fat from cooking juices; transfer back to pressure cooker. In a small bowl, mix the cornstarch and water until smooth; stir into cooking juices. Select saute setting and adjust for low heat. Simmer, stirring constantly, until thickened, 1-2 minutes. Serve with mashed potatoes, meat and vegetables.

FREEZE OPTION: Place the roast and vegetables in freezer containers; top with cooking juices. Cool and freeze. To use, partially thaw in the refrigerator overnight. Heat through in a covered saucepan, stirring gently and adding a little broth if necessary.

4 OZ. COOKED BEEF WITH ⅔ CUP VEGETABLES AND ½ CUP GRAVY: 316 cal., 15g fat (5g sat. fat), 89mg chol., 373mg sod., 16g carb. (4g sugars, 4g fiber), 30g pro. **DIABETIC EXCHANGES:** 4 lean meat, 2 vegetable, 1½ fat.

BEEF ROAST WITH ASIAN BLACK BEAN SAUCE

I love stir-fry with black bean sauce. This recipe takes the same delicious flavor and combines it with fork-tender pot roast.
—Judy Lawson, Chelsea, MI

Prep: 25 min.
Cook: 70 min. + releasing
Makes: 10 servings

- 1 **boneless beef chuck roast (3 to 4 lbs.)**
- ½ **tsp. salt**
- ½ **tsp. pepper**
- 1 **Tbsp. olive oil**
- 1 **cup reduced-sodium beef broth**
- 1 **medium onion, cut into 1-in. pieces**
- ½ **lb. sliced fresh mushrooms**
- 8 **oz. fresh snow peas, trimmed**
- ¾ **cup Asian black bean sauce**
- 2 **Tbsp. cornstarch**
- 2 **Tbsp. cold water**
  Hot cooked rice
- 4 **green onions, sliced**

1. Halve roast; sprinkle with salt and pepper. Select saute or browning setting on a 6-qt. electric pressure cooker. Adjust for medium heat; add 1½ tsp. oil. When oil is hot, brown a roast half on all sides. Remove; repeat with remaining beef and 1½ tsp. oil.

2. Add beef broth to pressure cooker. Cook 2 minutes, stirring to loosen browned bits from the pan. Press cancel. Return all to pressure cooker; add onion.

3. Lock the lid and close pressure-release valve. Adjust to pressure-cook on high for 60 minutes. Let the pressure release naturally for 10 minutes; quick-release any remaining pressure. Press cancel. A thermometer inserted in beef should read at least 160°.

4. Remove roast; keep warm. Add mushrooms, snow peas and black bean sauce to pressure cooker. Select saute setting and adjust for low heat. Cook and stir until the vegetables are tender; 6-8 minutes.

5. In a small bowl, mix the cornstarch and cold water until smooth; stir into pressure cooker. Simmer, stirring constantly, until thickened, 1-2 minutes. Serve with roast, hot cooked rice and green onions.

1 SERVING: 286 cal., 14g fat (5g sat. fat), 89mg chol., 635mg sod., 9g carb. (4g sugars, 1g fiber), 29g pro. **DIABETIC EXCHANGES:** 4 lean meat, ½ starch, ½ fat.

BEEF & RICE CABBAGE ROLLS

My family can't wait for dinner when I'm serving my tasty cabbage rolls. The dish comes together easily and always satisfies.
—Lynn Bowen, Geraldine, AL

Prep: 45 min.
Cook: 20 min.
Makes: 6 servings

12 **cabbage leaves**
 1 **cup cooked brown rice**
 ¼ **cup finely chopped onion**
 1 **large egg, lightly beaten**
 ¼ **cup fat-free milk**
 ½ **tsp. salt**
 ¼ **tsp. pepper**
 1 **lb. lean ground beef (90% lean)**
 ½ **cup plus 2 Tbsp. water, divided**
 1 **can (8 oz.) tomato sauce**
 1 **Tbsp. brown sugar**
 1 **Tbsp. lemon juice**
 1 **tsp. Worcestershire sauce**
 2 **Tbsp. cornstarch**

1. In batches, cook cabbage in boiling water 3-5 minutes or until crisp-tender. Drain; cool slightly. Trim the thick vein from the bottom of each cabbage leaf, making a V-shaped cut.

2. In a large bowl, combine rice, onion, egg, milk, salt and pepper. Add beef; mix lightly but thoroughly. Place about ¼ cup beef mixture on each cabbage leaf. Pull together the cut edges of leaf to overlap; fold over filling. Fold in the sides and roll up.

3. Place trivet insert and ½ cup water in a 6-qt. electric pressure cooker. Set 6 rolls on the trivet, seam side down. In a bowl, mix tomato sauce, brown sugar, lemon juice and Worcestershire sauce; pour half the sauce over cabbage rolls. Top with remaining rolls and sauce.

4. Lock lid; close pressure-release valve. Adjust to pressure-cook on high for 15 minutes. Quick-release pressure. Press cancel. A thermometer inserted in the beef should read at least 160°.

5. Remove the rolls to a serving platter; keep warm. Remove trivet. In a small bowl, mix cornstarch and remaining 2 Tbsp. water until smooth; stir into pressure cooker. Select the saute setting and adjust for low heat. Simmer, stirring constantly, until thickened, 1-2 minutes. Serve with rolls.

2 CABBAGE ROLLS: 219 cal., 8g fat (3g sat. fat), 78mg chol., 446mg sod., 19g carb. (5g sugars, 2g fiber), 18g pro. **DIABETIC EXCHANGES:** 2 lean meat, 1 starch.

CARIBBEAN POT ROAST

This tropical dish is definitely an all-year recipe. Sweet potatoes, orange zest and baking cocoa are my surprise ingredients.
—Jenn Tidwell, Fair Oaks, CA

Prep: 30 min.
Cook: 55 min. + releasing
Makes: 10 servings

- 1 Tbsp. canola oil
- 1 boneless beef chuck roast (2½ lbs.), halved
- ½ cup water
- 2 medium sweet potatoes, cubed
- 2 large carrots, sliced
- 1 large onion, chopped
- ¼ cup chopped celery
- 1 can (15 oz.) tomato sauce
- 2 garlic cloves, minced
- 1 Tbsp. all-purpose flour
- 1 Tbsp. sugar
- 1 Tbsp. brown sugar
- 1 tsp. ground cumin
- ¾ tsp. salt
- ¾ tsp. ground coriander
- ¾ tsp. chili powder
- ¾ tsp. grated orange zest
- ¾ tsp. baking cocoa
- ½ tsp. dried oregano
- ⅛ tsp. ground cinnamon

1. Select the saute or browning setting on a 6-qt. electric pressure cooker. Adjust for medium heat; add 1½ tsp. oil. When the oil is hot, brown a roast half on all sides. Remove; repeat with remaining beef and oil.

2. Add water to pressure cooker. Cook 30 seconds, stirring to loosen browned bits from the pan. Press cancel. Place the sweet potatoes, carrots, onion and celery in pressure cooker; top with beef. Combine remaining ingredients; pour over top.

3. Lock lid; close pressure-release valve. Adjust to pressure-cook on high for 55 minutes. Let pressure release naturally. A thermometer inserted in beef should read at least 145°.

FREEZE OPTION: Place the pot roast and vegetables in freezer containers; top with cooking juices. Cool and freeze. To use, partially thaw in the refrigerator overnight. Heat through in a covered saucepan, stirring gently and adding a little water if necessary.

3 OZ. COOKED BEEF WITH ½ CUP VEGETABLE MIXTURE : 282 cal., 13g fat (4g sat. fat), 74mg chol., 442mg sod., 18g carb. (8g sugars, 3g fiber), 24g pro. **DIABETIC EXCHANGES:** 3 lean meat, 1 starch, 1 vegetable, ½ fat.

BEEFY CABBAGE & BEAN STEW

While we were on a small-group quilting retreat, a friend of mine surprised everyone with this wonderful stew for dinner. We all loved it and have since passed the recipe around for others to enjoy—now I'm passing it on to you.
—Melissa Glancy, La Grange, KY

Prep: 30 min.
Cook: 5 min.
Makes: 6 servings

- ½ lb. lean ground beef (90% lean)
- 3 cups shredded cabbage or angel hair coleslaw mix
- 1 can (16 oz.) red beans, rinsed and drained
- 1 can (14½ oz.) diced tomatoes, undrained
- 1 can (8 oz.) tomato sauce
- ¾ cup water
- ¾ cup salsa or picante sauce
- 1 medium green pepper, chopped
- 1 small onion, chopped
- 3 garlic cloves, minced
- 1 tsp. ground cumin
- ½ tsp. pepper

1. Select saute or browning setting on a 6-qt. electric pressure cooker; adjust for medium heat. Cook beef until no longer pink, 6-8 minutes, breaking into crumbles; drain. Press cancel. Return beef to pressure cooker.

2. Stir in the remaining ingredients. Lock lid; close pressure-release valve. Adjust to pressure-cook on high for 3 minutes. Quick-release pressure.

FREEZE OPTION: Freeze the cooled stew in freezer containers. To use, partially thaw in refrigerator overnight. Heat through in a saucepan, stirring occasionally and adding a little water if necessary.

1 CUP: 177 cal., 4g fat (1g sat. fat), 24mg chol., 591mg sod., 23g carb. (5g sugars, 7g fiber), 13g pro. **DIABETIC EXCHANGES:** 2 lean meat, 1 starch, 1 vegetable.

STEAK FAJITAS

I've enjoyed cooking since I was a girl growing up in the Southwest, and I think fajitas are an easy way to add some wallop to ho-hum dinner lineups. This simply delicious main dish is an excellent option if you're looking for something new to serve.
—Janie Reitz, Rochester, MN

Prep: 20 min.
Cook: 5 min.
Makes: 6 servings

- 2 Tbsp. canola oil
- 1½ lbs. beef top sirloin steak, cut into thin strips
- 1 large onion, julienned
- 1 large sweet red pepper, julienned
- 1 garlic clove, minced
- ½ cup reduced-sodium beef broth
- 2 Tbsp. lemon juice
- 1½ tsp. ground cumin
- 1 tsp. seasoned salt
- ½ tsp. chili powder
- ¼ to ½ tsp. crushed red pepper flakes
- 12 mini flour tortillas (5 in.), warmed
  Optional toppings: Shredded cheddar cheese, fresh cilantro leaves, sliced jalapeno pepper and avocado

1. Select saute or browning setting on a 6-qt. electric pressure cooker. Adjust for medium heat; add oil. When the oil is hot, brown beef. Press cancel. Place onions, peppers and garlic on meat. Top with broth, lemon juice and seasonings.

2. Lock lid; close pressure-release valve. Adjust to pressure-cook on high for 3 minutes. Quick-release the pressure. A thermometer inserted in beef should read at least 160°. Using tongs, serve with tortillas and toppings as desired.

2 FAJITAS: 337 cal., 14g fat (4g sat. fat), 46mg chol., 554mg sod., 21g carb. (2g sugars, 3g fiber), 28g pro. **DIABETIC EXCHANGES:** 4 lean meat, 1½ starch, 1 fat.

WHY YOU'LL LOVE IT...

"This recipe is truly fabulous! It's my go-to for fajitas and I use it for chicken, too. I'll even double the recipe, so there's extra to make quick-and-easy quesadillas for dinner the next night."
—MAMATRICIA, TASTEOFHOME.COM

SWISS STEAK

Swiss steak has a been a standby for family cooks for decades, and this fuss-free version promises to keep the dish popular for years to come. Best of all, it's low in calories and fat.
—Sarah Burks, Wathena, KS

Prep: 10 min.
Cook: 20 min.
Makes: 6 servings

1½ lbs. beef round steak, cut into 6 pieces
½ tsp. salt
¼ tsp. pepper
1 medium onion, cut into ¼-in. slices
1 celery rib, cut into ½-in. slices
2 cans (8 oz. each) tomato sauce

Sprinkle the steak with salt and pepper. Place the onion in a 6-qt. electric pressure cooker. Top with the celery, tomato sauce and steak. Lock lid; close pressure-release valve. Adjust to pressure-cook on high for 20 minutes. Let pressure release naturally for 5 minutes; quick-release any remaining pressure. A thermometer inserted in steak should read at least 145°.

1 SERVING: 167 cal., 4g fat (1g sat. fat), 63mg chol., 581mg sod., 6g carb. (2g sugars, 2g fiber), 27g pro. **DIABETIC EXCHANGES:** 3 lean meat, 1 vegetable.

ROUND STEAK ITALIANO

My mom used to make a similar version of this wonderful dish, and I've always enjoyed it. The gravy is especially dense and flavorful.
—Deanne Stephens, McMinnville, OR

Prep: 15 min.
Cook: 20 min.
Makes: 8 servings

- 2 lbs. beef top round steak
- 1 can (8 oz.) tomato sauce
- ½ cup reduced-sodium beef broth
- 2 Tbsp. onion soup mix
- 2 Tbsp. canola oil
- 2 Tbsp. red wine vinegar
- 1 tsp. ground oregano
- ½ tsp. garlic powder
- ¼ tsp. pepper
- 8 medium potatoes (7 to 8 oz. each)
- 1 Tbsp. cornstarch
- 1 Tbsp. cold water

1. Cut steak into serving-size pieces; place in a 6-qt. electric pressure cooker. In a large bowl, combine tomato sauce, broth, soup mix, oil, vinegar, oregano, garlic powder and pepper; pour over meat. Scrub and pierce potatoes; place over meat.

2. Lock lid; close pressure-release valve. Adjust to pressure-cook on high for 15 minutes. Quick-release pressure. Press cancel. A thermometer inserted into beef should read at least 160°. Remove meat and potatoes; keep warm.

3. For gravy, skim fat from cooking juices; return to pressure cooker. In a small bowl, mix cornstarch and cold water until smooth; stir into pressure cooker. Select the saute setting and adjust for low heat. Simmer, stirring constantly, until thickened, 1-2 minutes. Serve with meat and potatoes.

1 SERVING: 353 cal., 7g fat (2g sat. fat), 64mg chol., 357mg sod., 41g carb. (2g sugars, 5g fiber), 31g pro. **DIABETIC EXCHANGES:** 4 lean meat, 3 starch, ½ fat.

BEEF & BEANS

This deliciously spicy steak with beans and rice will have your family and friends asking for more. It's a perennial favorite in my recipe collection.
—Marie Leamon, Bethesda, MD

Prep: 10 min.
Cook: 15 min.
Makes: 8 servings

1½ lbs. boneless
   round steak
1 Tbsp. prepared mustard
1 Tbsp. chili powder
½ tsp. salt
¼ tsp. pepper
1 garlic clove, minced
2 cans (14½ oz. each)
   diced tomatoes,
   undrained
1 medium onion,
   chopped
½ cup water
1 tsp. beef bouillon
   granules
1 can (16 oz.) kidney
   beans, rinsed
   and drained
   Hot cooked rice

1. Cut steak into thin strips. Combine mustard, chili powder, salt, pepper and garlic in a bowl; add steak and toss to coat. Transfer to a 6-qt. electric pressure cooker; add tomatoes, onion, water and bouillon.

2. Lock lid; close pressure-release valve. Adjust to pressure-cook on high for 15 minutes. Quick-release pressure. Stir in the beans; heat through. Serve with rice.

1 CUP: 185 cal., 3g fat (1g sat. fat), 48mg chol., 574mg sod., 16g carb. (5g sugars, 5g fiber), 24g pro. **DIABETIC EXCHANGES:** 3 lean meat, 1 starch.

DID YOU KNOW?
Canned beans are packed with a lot of sodium in order to extend their shelf life. Be sure to rinse and drain the beans before using them in recipes.

SOUPS & SANDWICHES

Who can resist the incomparable pairing
of soup and sandwich? Now you don't have to,
regardless of your healthy-eating goals. Let your
one-pot cooker do the work and settle in for
a delectable duo of flavor.

CLASSIC COMBO NEVER FAILS

Cutting calories and fat doesn't have to mean missing out on soups and sandwiches. Read up on these definitions and pointers for meal planning made easy.

STOCK
Usually made with meaty bones (possibly roasted), meat and vegetables. Stock is clear and free of fat, offering a very subtle flavor.

CONSOMME
A completely defatted and clarified stock. It has a very rich flavor and, because of its high gelatin content, will set up when chilled.

BROTH
A light, thin soup made from simmering meats, poultry, fish or vegetables. Broths and stocks may be used interchangeably, but broths have less body.

CHILI
A hearty dish usually made with tomatoes and chili powder, but some chili dishes are white. The variations on chili seem endless. A chili can be mild, hot or anywhere in between. It may include ground beef, stew meat, sausage or poultry, or be meatless.

CREAMED SOUP
Pureed soup with a smooth, silky texture. Most focus on a single vegetable. It may be thickened with flour or potatoes and can be made with or without cream.

GUMBO
A hearty stewlike soup usually served with white rice that starts with a dark roux of flour and oil or butter. It may contain shellfish, chicken, sausage, ham, tomatoes, onions, garlic, sweet peppers and/or celery. Okra is used as a thickening agent in addition to the roux.

SECRETS TO KEEPING SOUPS LIGHT

- Skip the salt. Use fresh herbs or salt-free seasoning to liven up flavor.

- Garnish soup with chopped fresh herbs, sliced green onions or diced vegetables instead of croutons, nuts, crackers, shredded cheese or crumbled bacon.

- For a golden yellow color in chicken or turkey soup, add a dash of turmeric.

- Store healthy soups in the freezer for quick meals, but note that those made with potatoes, fruit, cream, yogurt, eggs or milk do not freeze well.

- Lentils, rice, barley and pasta continue to absorb liquid after cooking. When reheating the soup, you may need a bit of water or even a bit of low-sodium broth for thinning.

DO YOU HAVE TO SOAK BEANS WHEN USING A PRESSURE COOKER FOR SOUP?

Soaking beans overnight—or using the quick-soak technique—is so well ingrained in our minds that it's become a given. But do you really need to take this step when cooking with a pressure cooker?

Almost any from-scratch bean recipe starts with the same instructions: Soak beans in cold water overnight, or use the quicker method and soak them in warm water for an hour. You may have noticed that not all pressure-cooker recipes call for the standard soaking. Feeling confused? Don't be!

The high temperatures reached inside electric pressure cookers dramatically decrease the cooking time of beans. They may cook as much as 75 percent faster! That's why many recipes might skip the soaking step. The beans can cook from a dried state in the time it takes a tough cut of meat to tenderize.

Keep in mind that thin-skinned beans such as black-eyed peas, pintos and black beans yield the best results when you skip the soak method. If you want to speed things up, though, using canned or presoaked beans always results in a fully cooked pressure-cooker soup without much fuss.

SANDWICH PIZAZZ

Add a little extra punch to ordinary sandwiches, wraps and pitas by replacing the butter or full-fat mayo with one of these quick-to-fix spreads.

GARLIC MAYO — Microwave 8 peeled garlic cloves and 1 tsp. olive oil, uncovered, on high for 20-30 seconds or until garlic is softened. Transfer to a blender. Add 1 Tbsp. each lemon juice and Dijon mustard, ¾ cup light mayonnaise and 2 Tbsp. plain fat-free yogurt; cover and process until blended.

MAYO WITH A KICK — Mix ⅓ cup light mayonnaise with ⅓-½ tsp. prepared horseradish, ½ tsp. minced chives and ¼-½ tsp. garlic powder.

BLAZING MUSTARD — Combine ½ cup ground mustard, 1½ tsp. sugar and ½ tsp. salt. Stir in 3 Tbsp. water and 2 Tbsp. white vinegar until smooth.

ARTICHOKE PEPPERONCINI SANDWICH SPREAD — Process ⅓ cup rinsed and drained water-packed artichoke hearts with 2 whole pepperoncini peppers in a food processor until spreadable but not smooth.

CHIMICHURRI SANDWICH SPREAD — Whisk together 2 Tbsp. olive oil, 1 Tbsp. each red wine vinegar, minced onion and minced fresh cilantro, 1 minced garlic clove, ¼ tsp. dried oregano and ⅛ tsp. each salt and cayenne pepper.

SUN-DRIED TOMATO SPREAD — Mix 2 Tbsp. each mayonnaise and finely chopped oil-packed sun-dried tomatoes and 2 tsp. minced red onion.

THE EASIEST EGG SALAD SANDWICHES EVER!

Once you use a pressure cooker to hard-boil eggs for egg salad, you'll never want to go back!

- Place 1 cup of water in a pressure cooker. Place a steamer basket or trivet insert on top of the water and carefully place up to 12 eggs on top.

- Lock lid; close pressure-release valve. Adjust to pressure-cook on high (for large eggs), and set time for 5 minutes. Meanwhile, prepare an ice bath.

- When cooking is complete, allow pressure to naturally release for 5 minutes. Quick-release any remaining pressure. Open cooker; transfer the eggs to the ice bath to cool for 5 minutes. Peel eggs when ready to create your egg salad.

LAMB PITAS WITH YOGURT SAUCE

The spiced lamb in these stuffed pita pockets goes perfectly with cool cucumber and yogurt. It's like having your own Greek gyro stand in the kitchen!
—Angela Leinenbach, Mechanicsville, VA

Prep: 25 min.
Cook: 15 min. + releasing
Makes: 8 servings

- 2 Tbsp. olive oil
- 2 lbs. lamb stew meat (¾-in. pieces)
- ½ cup dry red wine
- 1 large onion, chopped
- 1 garlic clove, minced
- 1¼ tsp. salt, divided
- 1 tsp. dried oregano
- ½ tsp. dried basil
- ⅓ cup tomato paste
- 1 medium cucumber
- 1 cup plain yogurt
- 16 pita pocket halves, warmed
- 4 plum tomatoes, sliced

DID YOU KNOW?
You can buy lamb when it's on sale and freeze it for a later date. Allow at least 24 hours for lamb stew meat to defrost.

1. Select saute or browning setting on a 6-qt. electric pressure cooker. Adjust for medium heat; add the oil. When oil is hot, brown lamb in batches. Add wine to pressure cooker. Cook 30 seconds, stirring to loosen browned bits from pan. Press cancel. Add onion, garlic, 1 tsp. salt, oregano and basil. Return lamb to pressure cooker.

2. Lock lid; close pressure-release valve. Adjust to pressure-cook on high for 15 minutes. Let pressure release naturally for 10 minutes; quick-release any remaining pressure. Press cancel.

3. Select saute setting; adjust for low heat. Add the tomato paste; simmer, uncovered, until mixture is slightly thickened, 8-10 minutes, stirring occasionally. Press cancel.

4. To serve, dice enough cucumber to measure 1 cup; thinly slice remaining cucumber. Combine diced cucumber with yogurt and remaining salt. Fill pitas with the lamb mixture, tomatoes, sliced cucumbers and yogurt mixture.

FREEZE OPTION: Freeze the cooled lamb mixture in freezer containers. To use, partially thaw in refrigerator overnight. Heat through in a saucepan, stirring occasionally and adding a little broth or water if necessary.

2 FILLED PITA HALVES: 383 cal., 11g fat (3g sat. fat), 78mg chol., 766mg sod., 39g carb. (5g sugars, 3g fiber), 31g pro. **DIABETIC EXCHANGES:** 3 lean meat, 2½ starch, 1 fat.

VEGETABLE WILD RICE SOUP

This thick and hearty soup is packed with colorful vegetables. It's wonderful for lunch alongside a healthy salad or light sandwich.
—Thomas Faglon, Somerset, NJ

Prep: 25 min.
Cook: 20 min. + releasing
Makes: 12 servings (3 qt.)

- 6 cups reduced-sodium vegetable broth
- 2 cans (14½ oz. each) fire-roasted diced tomatoes, undrained
- 2 celery ribs, sliced
- 2 medium carrots, chopped
- 1¾ cups baby portobello mushrooms, sliced
- 1 medium onion, chopped
- 1 medium parsnip, peeled and chopped
- 1 medium sweet potato, peeled and cubed
- 1 medium green pepper, chopped
- 1 cup uncooked wild rice
- 2 garlic cloves, minced
- ¾ tsp. salt
- ¼ tsp. pepper
- 2 bay leaves
- 2 fresh thyme sprigs

1. Combine all ingredients in a 6-qt. electric pressure cooker. Lock lid; close pressure-release valve. Adjust to pressure-cook on high for 20 minutes. Let pressure release naturally for 10 minutes; quick-release any remaining pressure.

2. Discard the bay leaves and thyme sprigs before serving. If desired, serve with additional thyme.

FREEZE OPTION: Freeze the cooled soup in freezer containers. To use, partially thaw in refrigerator overnight. Heat through in a saucepan, stirring occasionally and adding a little broth if necessary.

1 CUP: 117 cal., 0 fat (0 sat. fat), 0 chol., 419mg sod., 25g carb. (7g sugars, 4g fiber), 4g pro. **DIABETIC EXCHANGES:** 2 vegetable, 1 starch.

MEXICAN SHREDDED BEEF WRAPS

The first time I served these wrap sandwiches was at the party after my son's baptism. Everyone liked them so much that it's become one of my go-to party recipes.
—Amy Lents, Grand Forks, ND

Prep: 20 min.
Cook: 50 min. + releasing
Makes: 6 servings

- 1 **boneless beef chuck roast (2 to 3 lbs.), halved**
- ½ **tsp. salt**
- ½ **tsp. pepper**
- 1 **small onion, finely chopped**
- 1 **jalapeno pepper, seeded and minced**
- 3 **garlic cloves, minced**
- 1 **can (8 oz.) tomato sauce**
- ½ **cup water**
- ¼ **cup lime juice**
- 1 **Tbsp. chili powder**
- 1 **tsp. ground cumin**
- ¼ **tsp. cayenne pepper**
- 6 **flour or whole wheat tortillas (8 in.)**
  Optional toppings:
    Torn romaine, chopped tomatoes, sliced avocado and sour cream

1. Sprinkle roast with salt and pepper; place in a 6-qt. electric pressure cooker. Top with onion, jalapeno pepper and garlic. In a small bowl, mix tomato sauce, water, lime juice, chili powder, cumin and cayenne; pour over roast. Lock lid; close pressure-release valve. Adjust to pressure-cook on high for 50 minutes. Let pressure release naturally. A thermometer inserted in beef should read at least 145°.

2. Remove roast; cool slightly. Shred meat with 2 forks; return to pressure cooker. Serve beef on tortillas with the toppings of your choice.

FREEZE OPTION: Freeze the cooled meat mixture and juices in freezer containers. To use, partially thaw in refrigerator overnight. Heat through in a saucepan, stirring occasionally and adding a little water if necessary.

1 WRAP: 440 cal., 18g fat (6g sat. fat), 98mg chol., 707mg sod., 33g carb. (2g sugars, 3g fiber), 35g pro. **DIABETIC EXCHANGES:** 5 lean meat, 2 starch.

BLACK BEAN SOUP

Life can get really crazy with young children, but I never want to compromise when it comes to cooking. This recipe is healthy and so easy thanks to my one-pot cooker!
—Angela Lemoine, Howell, NJ

Prep: 20 min.
Cook: 5 min. + releasing
Makes: 6 cups

- 1 tsp. olive oil
- 1 cup fresh or frozen corn
- 2 cans (15 oz. each) black beans, rinsed and drained
- 2 cans (14½ oz. each) vegetable broth
- 1 medium onion, finely chopped
- 1 medium sweet red pepper, finely chopped
- 4 garlic cloves, minced
- 2 tsp. ground cumin
  Dash pepper
  Minced fresh cilantro

1. Select saute or browning setting on a 6-qt. electric pressure cooker. Adjust for medium heat; add oil. When oil is hot, add corn. Cook and stir until golden brown, 4-6 minutes. Press cancel. Remove corn and keep warm. Add beans, vegetable broth, onion, red pepper, garlic and cumin to pressure cooker.

2. Lock lid; close pressure-release valve. Adjust to pressure-cook on high for 5 minutes. Let pressure release naturally for 10 minutes; quick-release any remaining pressure.

3. Puree soup using an immersion blender, or cool soup slightly and puree in batches in a blender. Return to pressure cooker; heat through. Sprinkle soup with pepper. Garnish with reserved corn and cilantro.

FREEZE OPTION: Freeze the cooled soup in freezer containers. To use, partially thaw in refrigerator overnight. Heat through in a saucepan, stirring occasionally and adding a little broth if necessary. Sprinkle with toppings.

¾ **CUP:** 125 cal., 1g fat (0 sat. fat), 0 chol., 517mg sod., 22g carb. (4g sugars, 5g fiber), 6g pro. **DIABETIC EXCHANGES:** 1½ starch.

BEEF & VEGGIE SLOPPY JOES

Because I'm always looking for new ways to serve my family healthy and delicious food, I started experimenting with my go-to veggies and ground beef. I came up with this favorite that my kids actually request!
—Megan Niebuhr, Yakima, WA

Prep: 35 min.
Cook: 5 min.
Makes: 10 servings

- 2 lbs. lean ground beef (90% lean)
- 4 medium carrots, shredded
- 1 medium yellow summer squash, shredded
- 1 medium zucchini, shredded
- 1 medium sweet red pepper, finely chopped
- 2 medium tomatoes, seeded and chopped
- 1 small red onion, finely chopped
- ½ cup ketchup
- ¼ cup water
- 3 Tbsp. minced fresh basil or 3 tsp. dried basil
- 2 Tbsp. cider vinegar
- 2 garlic cloves, minced
- ½ tsp. salt
- ½ tsp. pepper
- 3 Tbsp. molasses
- 10 whole wheat hamburger buns, split

1. Select saute or browning setting on a 6-qt. electric pressure cooker; adjust for medium heat. Cook beef until no longer pink, 8-10 minutes, breaking into crumbles; drain. Return to pressure cooker. Add carrots, summer squash, zucchini, red pepper, tomatoes, onion, ketchup, water, basil, vinegar, garlic, salt and pepper (do not stir).

2. Lock lid; close pressure-release valve. Adjust to pressure-cook on high for 5 minutes. Quick-release pressure. Stir in molasses. Using a slotted spoon, serve beef mixture on buns.

FREEZE OPTION: Freeze the cooled meat mixture and juices in freezer containers. To use, partially thaw in refrigerator overnight. Heat through in a saucepan, stirring occasionally and adding a little water if necessary.

1 SANDWICH: 316 cal., 10g fat (3g sat. fat), 57mg chol., 566mg sod., 36g carb. (15g sugars, 5g fiber), 22g pro. **DIABETIC EXCHANGES:** 3 lean meat, 2½ starch.

TEST KITCHEN TIP
This recipe is a great way to work more veggies into your family's mealtime lineup. For an extra nutrition and flavor boost, stir several tablespoons of canned pumpkin into the meat mixture just before serving.

GREEK-STYLE LENTIL SOUP

This is a nice warming soup on a chilly day. Lentils are so good for you, too!
—Mary E. Smith, Columbia, MO

Prep: 20 min.
Cook: 15 min. + releasing
Makes: 12 servings (3 qt.)

- 4 **cups water**
- 4 **cups vegetable broth**
- 2 **cups dried lentils, rinsed**
- 2 **medium carrots, chopped**
- 1 **small onion, chopped**
- 1 **celery rib, chopped**
- 2 **garlic cloves, minced**
- 1 **tsp. dried oregano**
- 1 **cup chopped fresh spinach**
- ½ **cup tomato sauce**
- 1 **can (2¼ oz.) sliced ripe olives, drained**
- 3 **Tbsp. red wine vinegar**
- ½ **tsp. salt**
- ¼ **tsp. pepper**
  Optional toppings:
  Chopped red onion, chopped parsley and lemon wedges

1. Place the water, broth, lentils, carrots, onion, celery, garlic and oregano in a 6-qt. electric pressure cooker. Lock lid; close pressure-release valve. Adjust to pressure cook on high for 15 minutes. Let pressure release naturally for 10 minutes; quick-release any remaining pressure.

2. Stir in spinach, tomato sauce, ripe olives, red wine vinegar, salt and pepper. If desired, serve with red onion, parsley and lemon wedges.

FREEZE OPTION: Freeze the cooled soup in freezer containers. To use, partially thaw in refrigerator overnight. Heat through in a saucepan, stirring occasionally and adding a little broth if necessary.

1 CUP: 134 cal., 1g fat (0 sat. fat), 0 chol., 420mg sod., 24g carb. (2g sugars, 4g fiber), 9g pro. **DIABETIC EXCHANGES:** 1½ starch, 1 lean meat.

ITALIAN BEEF SANDWICHES

With only a few ingredients, these roast beef sandwiches are a snap to throw together. The meat turns out wonderfully tender.
—Lauren Adamson, Layton, UT

Prep: 10 min.
Cook: 1 hour + releasing
Makes: 12 servings

- 1 jar (16 oz.) sliced pepperoncini, undrained
- 1 can (14½ oz.) diced tomatoes, undrained
- 1 medium onion, chopped
- ½ cup water
- 2 pkg. Italian salad dressing mix
- 1 tsp. dried oregano
- ½ tsp. garlic powder
- 1 beef rump roast or bottom round roast (3 to 4 lbs.)
- 12 Italian rolls, split

1. In a bowl, mix the first 7 ingredients. Halve beef roast; place in a 6-qt. electric pressure cooker. Pour pepperoncini mixture over the top. Lock lid; close pressure-release valve. Adjust to pressure-cook on high for 60 minutes. Let pressure release naturally. A thermometer inserted into beef should read at least 145°.

2. Remove roast; cool slightly. Skim fat from cooking juices. Shred beef with 2 forks. Return beef and cooking juices to pressure cooker; heat through. Serve on rolls.

TO MAKE AHEAD: In a large shallow freezer container, combine the first 7 ingredients. Add roast; cover and freeze. To use, place freezer container in refrigerator 48 hours or until roast is completely thawed. Cook and serve as directed.

FREEZE OPTION: Freeze cooled, cooked beef mixture in freezer containers. To use, partially thaw in refrigerator overnight. Heat through in a saucepan, stirring occasionally and adding a little water if necessary.

1 SANDWICH: 278 cal., 7g fat (2g sat. fat), 67mg chol., 735mg sod., 24g carb. (3g sugars, 2g fiber), 26g pro. **DIABETIC EXCHANGES:** 3 lean meat, 1½ starch.

TURKEY CHILI

I took my mother's milder recipe for chili and made it thicker and more robust. It's a favorite, especially in fall and winter.
—Celesta Zanger, Bloomfield Hills, MI

Prep: 20 min.
Cook: 5 min. + releasing
Makes: 12 servings (3 qt.)

- 1 lb. lean ground turkey
- 1½ cups water
- 2 cans (14½ oz. each) no-salt-added diced tomatoes, undrained
- 1 jar (24 oz.) meatless pasta sauce
- 1 can (16 oz.) hot chili beans, undrained
- 1 can (16 oz.) kidney beans, rinsed and drained
- 1 can (15 oz.) pinto beans, rinsed and drained
- ¾ cup chopped celery
- ¾ cup chopped onion
- ¾ cup chopped green pepper
- ½ cup frozen corn
- 2 Tbsp. chili powder
- 1 tsp. ground cumin
- ¼ tsp. pepper
- ⅛ to ¼ tsp. cayenne pepper
  Optional toppings: Sour cream, cubed avocado, diced jalapeno peppers

1. Select saute or browning setting on a 6-qt. electric pressure cooker; adjust for medium heat. Cook turkey until no longer pink, 6-8 minutes, breaking up turkey into crumbles; drain. Add the water to pressure cooker. Cook 1 minute, stirring to loosen browned bits from pan. Return turkey to pressure cooker. Stir in tomatoes, pasta sauce, beans, celery, onion, green pepper, corn and seasonings.

2. Lock lid; close pressure-release valve. Adjust to pressure-cook on high for 5 minutes. Let pressure release naturally for 10 minutes; quick-release any remaining pressure. If desired, serve with sour cream, avocado and jalapeno.

FREEZE OPTION: Freeze cooled chili in freezer containers. To use, partially thaw in refrigerator overnight. Heat through in a saucepan, stirring occasionally and adding a little water if necessary.

1 CUP: 200 cal., 4g fat (1g sat. fat), 26mg chol., 535mg sod., 29g carb. (8g sugars, 8g fiber), 15g pro. **DIABETIC EXCHANGES:** 2 lean meat, 2 vegetable, 1 starch.

TEST KITCHEN TIP
Want to trim down this recipe even more? Replace the ground turkey with vegetarian crumbles. Found in the frozen food aisle, these meat-free bits are ideal in robust dishes like chili and spaghetti sauce.

TANDOORI CHICKEN PANINI

Tandoori-style spices give this a bold flavor that's hard to resist. The shredded chicken tastes incredible tucked between pieces of naan, then grilled for an Indian-inspired panini.
—Yasmin Arif, Manassas, VA

Prep: 25 min.
Cook: 10 min.
Makes: 6 servings

1½ lbs. boneless skinless chicken breasts
½ cup reduced-sodium chicken broth
2 garlic cloves, minced
2 tsp. minced fresh gingerroot
1 tsp. paprika
¼ tsp. salt
¼ to ½ tsp. cayenne pepper
¼ tsp. ground turmeric
6 green onions, chopped
6 Tbsp. chutney
6 naan flatbreads

1. Place the first 8 ingredients in a 6-qt. electric pressure cooker. Lock lid; close pressure-release valve. Adjust to pressure-cook on high for 6 minutes. Quick-release pressure. A thermometer inserted in chicken should read at least 165°.

2. Remove chicken; shred with 2 forks. Return to pressure cooker. Stir in green onions; heat through.

3. Spread chutney over 1 side of each naan. Using a slotted spoon, top chutney side of 3 naan with chicken mixture; top with remaining naan, chutney side down.

4. Cook the sandwiches on a panini maker or indoor grill until golden brown, 6-8 minutes. To serve, cut each sandwich in half.

FREEZE OPTION: Freeze the cooled meat mixture and juices in freezer containers. To use, partially thaw in refrigerator overnight. Heat through in a saucepan, stirring occasionally and adding a little broth if necessary.

½ **SANDWICH:** 351 cal., 6g fat (2g sat. fat), 68mg chol., 853mg sod., 44g carb. (13g sugars, 2g fiber), 28g pro.

ENGLISH PUB SPLIT PEA SOUP

This family favorite is the same recipe my grandmother used. With the magic of today's appliances, I can put it together in just 15 minutes, walk away for a bit and then it's "soup's on!" Finish it with more milk if you like your soup a little thinner.
—Judy Batson, Tampa, FL

Prep: 15 min.
Cook: 15 min. + releasing
Makes: 8 servings (2 qt.)

- 1 meaty ham bone
- 4 cups water
- 1 bottle (12 oz.) light beer
- 1⅓ cups dried green split peas, rinsed
- 2 celery ribs, chopped
- 1 large carrot, chopped
- 1 sweet onion, chopped
- 1 Tbsp. prepared English mustard
- ½ cup 2% milk
- ¼ cup minced fresh parsley
- ½ tsp. salt
- ¼ tsp. pepper
- ¼ tsp. ground nutmeg

1. Place ham bone in a 6-qt. electric pressure cooker. Add water, beer, peas, celery, carrot, onion and mustard. Lock lid; close pressure-release valve. Adjust to pressure-cook on high for 15 minutes. Let pressure release naturally.

2. Remove bone from soup. Cool slightly, trim away fat and remove meat from bone; discard fat and bone. Cut meat into bite-sized pieces; return to pressure cooker. Stir in remaining ingredients. If desired, top with additional minced parsley.

1 CUP: 188 cal., 2g fat (1g sat. fat), 22mg chol., 622mg sod., 26g carb. (6g sugars, 9g fiber), 16g pro. **DIABETIC EXCHANGES:** 1½ starch, 1 lean meat.

ITALIAN PULLED PORK SANDWICHES

Enjoy all the flavors of Italian sausage sandwiches with this healthier alternative.
—Mike Dellario, Middleport, NY

Prep: 20 min.
Cook: 45 min. + releasing
Makes: 12 servings

- 1 Tbsp. fennel seed, crushed
- 1 Tbsp. steak seasoning
- 1 tsp. cayenne pepper, optional
- 1 boneless pork shoulder butt roast (3 lbs.)
- 1 Tbsp. olive oil
- 2 medium green or sweet red peppers, thinly sliced
- 2 medium onions, thinly sliced
- 1 can (14½ oz.) diced tomatoes, undrained
- ½ cup water
- 12 whole wheat hamburger buns, split

1. In a small bowl, combine fennel seed, steak seasoning and cayenne if desired. Cut roast in half. Rub seasoning mixture over pork. Select saute or browning setting on a 6-qt. electric pressure cooker. Adjust for medium heat; add oil. When oil is hot, brown a roast half on all sides. Remove; repeat with remaining pork. Press cancel.

2. Return all to pressure cooker. Add the peppers, onions, tomatoes and water. Lock lid; close pressure-release valve. Adjust to pressure-cook on high for 45 minutes. Let pressure release naturally. A thermometer inserted in pork should read at least 145°.

3. Remove pork roast; shred with 2 forks. Strain cooking juices; skim fat. Return cooking juices, vegetables and pork to pressure cooker; heat through. Using a slotted spoon, serve pork mixture on buns.

FREEZE OPTION: Freeze the cooled meat mixture and juices in freezer containers. To use, partially thaw in refrigerator overnight. Heat through in a saucepan, stirring occasionally and adding a little water if necessary.

1 SANDWICH: 285 cal., 9g fat (2g sat. fat), 57mg chol., 483mg sod., 27g carb. (6g sugars, 5g fiber), 26g pro. **DIABETIC EXCHANGES:** 3 lean meat, 2 starch, ½ fat.

TURKEY VEGETABLE SOUP

Our family is big on soup. This tasty favorite is quick to make, giving me plenty of time to have fun with the family before we dig in.
—Nancy Heishman, Las Vegas, NV

Prep: 30 min.
Cook: 5 min. + releasing
Makes: 10 servings (3½ qt.)

- 1 pkg. (19½ oz.) Italian turkey sausage links, casings removed
- 3 large tomatoes, chopped
- 1 can (15 oz.) garbanzo beans or chickpeas, rinsed and drained
- 3 medium carrots, thinly sliced
- 1½ cups cut fresh green beans (1-in. pieces)
- 1 medium zucchini, quartered lengthwise and sliced
- 1 large sweet red or green pepper, chopped
- 8 green onions, chopped
- 4 cups chicken stock
- 1 can (12 oz.) tomato paste
- ½ tsp. seasoned salt
- ⅓ cup minced fresh basil

1. Select saute or browning setting on a 6-qt. electric pressure cooker; adjust for medium heat. Cook sausage until no longer pink, 6-8 minutes, breaking into crumbles; drain. Return to pressure cooker. Press cancel.

2. Add tomatoes, beans, carrots, green beans, zucchini, pepper and onions. In a large bowl, whisk stock, tomato paste and seasoned salt; pour over the vegetables. Lock lid; close pressure-release valve. Adjust to pressure-cook on high for 5 minutes. Let pressure release naturally for 10 minutes; quick-release any remaining pressure. Just before serving, stir in basil.

FREEZE OPTION: Freeze cooled soup in freezer containers. To use, partially thaw in refrigerator overnight. Heat through in a saucepan, stirring occasionally and adding a little stock if necessary.

1⅓ **CUPS:** 167 cal., 5g fat (1g sat. fat), 20mg chol., 604mg sod., 21g carb. (9g sugars, 5g fiber), 13g pro. **DIABETIC EXCHANGES:** 2 lean meat, 2 vegetable, ½ starch.

SHREDDED CHICKEN GYROS

Our family has no ties of any kind to Greece, but we always have such a marvelous time at the annual Salt Lake City Greek Festival. One of my favorite parts is the awesome food. This meal is a good way to mix up our menu, and my kids are big fans.
—Camille Beckstrand, Layton, UT

Prep: 20 min.
Cook: 10 min.
Makes: 8 servings

2 medium onions, chopped
6 garlic cloves, minced
1 tsp. lemon-pepper seasoning
1 tsp. dried oregano
½ tsp. ground allspice
½ cup lemon juice
¼ cup red wine vinegar
2 Tbsp. olive oil
2 lbs. boneless skinless chicken breasts
8 whole pita breads
    Toppings: Tzatziki sauce, torn romaine and sliced tomato, cucumber and onion

1. In a 6-qt. electric pressure cooker, combine the first 8 ingredients; add chicken. Lock lid; close pressure-release valve. Adjust to pressure-cook on high for 6 minutes. Quick-release pressure. A thermometer inserted in chicken should read at least 165°.

2. Remove chicken; shred with 2 forks. Return to pressure cooker. Using tongs, place chicken mixture on pita breads. Serve with toppings.

FREEZE OPTION: Freeze the cooled meat mixture and juices in freezer containers. To use, partially thaw in refrigerator overnight. Heat through in a saucepan, stirring occasionally and adding a little water if necessary.

1 GYRO: 335 cal., 7g fat (1g sat. fat), 63mg chol., 418mg sod., 38g carb. (2g sugars, 2g fiber), 29g pro. **DIABETIC EXCHANGES:** 3 lean meat, 2½ starch, ½ fat.

CREAMY CAULIFLOWER SOUP

I love indulgent cream soups but not the fat that goes along with them. The velvety texture of this healthier cauliflower soup makes it feel so rich, and the spicy kick warms you from the inside out.
—Teri Rasey, Cadillac, MI

Prep: 20 min.
Cook: 5 min. + releasing
Makes: 14 servings (3½ qt.)

6 cups water
1¾ lbs. Yukon Gold potatoes (about 4 medium), peeled and cut into 1-in. cubes
1 medium head cauliflower (about 1½ lbs.), cut into 1-in. pieces
1 small onion, chopped
3 garlic cloves, minced
1 large bay leaf
3 tsp. dried celery flakes
1½ tsp. salt
1½ tsp. adobo seasoning
¾ tsp. ground mustard
¼ tsp. cayenne pepper
¾ cup nonfat dry milk powder
Optional toppings: Shredded cheddar cheese, sliced green onions and croutons

1. Place water, vegetables and seasonings in a 6-qt. electric pressure cooker. Lock lid; close pressure-release valve. Adjust to pressure-cook on high for 5 minutes. Let pressure release naturally for 10 minutes; quick-release any remaining pressure.

2. Discard bay leaf. Stir in milk powder until dissolved. Puree soup using an immersion blender. Or, cool slightly and puree soup in batches in a blender; return to pressure cooker and heat through. If desired, serve with toppings.

1 CUP: 80 cal., 0 fat (0 sat. fat), 1mg chol., 434mg sod., 17g carb. (4g sugars, 2g fiber), 3g pro. **DIABETIC EXCHANGES:** 1 vegetable, ½ starch.

SWEETS & DESSERTS

If it's a treat you're craving, you've come to the right spot. High on flavor and low in calories, fat and sugar, these specialties satisfy everyone. Best of all, you don't have to be a baker. Your electric pressure cooker does the work for you!

MAKING ROOM FOR DESSERT

Eating right doesn't mean giving up on after-dinner treats that make meals special. When comes to light desserts that satisfy your cravings, you can't go wrong with fruit, a handful of kitchen staples and your electric pressure cooker. Review the tips and hints here, then see the delectable lineup of delightful treats that follows.

FRUIT	HOW TO BUY	HOW TO STORE	HOW TO PREP
APPLES	Deep colors indicate that an apple has absorbed lots of sunlight. Give apples a squeeze; they should be firm with no give. Also inspect them for blemishes or dents, as these can accelerate decay.	Store in a cool place. If storing in the refrigerator place apples, in a bag with holes in it, in the crisper bin. Remove any damaged apples so rot does not spread. Don't store other fruits or vegetables in the same drawer; apples give off ethylene gas, which causes produce to rot faster.	Always wash apples (especially nonorganic ones) before eating or prepping for use in a recipe. Use 1 tsp. of baking soda to 2 cups of water as a wash; this has been shown to remove the majority of trace pesticides from apple skin.
PEARS	Select pears that are plump. Avoid those with bruises, soft spots or cuts. For some varieties, the color of the skin will change as the pear ripens. Select firm pears for baking. For eating, select pears that give slightly when gently pressed.	Store unwashed ripe pears in the refrigerator for 3-5 days, away from other fruits and vegetables with strong aromas. To ripen firm pears, place them in a paper bag at room temperature for 2-3 days.	Wash before using. Peel if desired and eat whole, sliced or chopped. When preparing pears for a recipe, brush the cut flesh with lemon juice to prevent browning. For pressure cooking, choose pears that are slightly underripe.
BERRIES	Select berries that are plump; avoid those that are bruised, mushy or moldy. Avoid packages with juice-stained bottoms.	Fragile berries are highly perishable. Store the unwashed berries in their container for 1-2 days. To freeze, wash berries and drain well; arrange in a single layer on a parchment-lined baking sheet. Once frozen, transfer to a freezer container. Freeze berries for up to 1 year.	Gently wash berries before using. Eat them on their own or follow the recipe's directions for slicing, chopping or pureeing.
PEACHES	Select peaches and nectarines that are firm but yield a bit to gentle pressure. They should be bright with skin free of discoloration, soft spots or bruises. Choose fruits with defined clefts, as this indicates they are mature and sweeter.	Both peaches and nectarines can be stored unrefrigerated for up to 4 days, depending on how ripe they were when you bought them. Keeping your peaches at room temperature offers a fuller, more intense flavor.	Give the fruit a light rinse; scrubbing will remove its delicate skin. Fully slice the fruit lengthwise. Take the two halves and twist. A ripe peach will easily come apart in two halves, exposing the pit, which you can then pluck out.
PUMPKIN	Choose a pumpkin that has even color saturation. It should be firm and feel heavy for its size. Pie pumpkins are smaller than the "jack-o'-lantern" type and make flavorful puree for use in pies, cakes and other baked goods.	Pumpkin and other winter squash keeps very well; simply store it in a cool, dark place, such as the inside of a cabinet or kitchen pantry, and it will last for up to 1 month.	Rinse the pumpkin or other squash and cut it lengthwise, scooping out the fibrous section and seeds. If you like, microwave the squash for 3-4 minutes before cutting. This softens the skin and makes it easier to slice.

THE SPICE OF LIFE

Pumpkin pie spice is a wonderful way to add some heartwarming comfort to most any dessert--without adding fat or sugar. If you're out of the popular spice, it's easy to make your own. Simply mix 4 tsp. ground cinnamon, 2 tsp. ground ginger, 1 tsp. ground cloves and ½ tsp. ground nutmeg. Store in an airtight container in a cool, dry place up to 6 months.

▼ GINGER
2 TSP.

▲ CINNAMON
4 TSP.

▲ CLOVES
1 TSP.

▲ NUTMEG
½ TSP.

CUT LIKE A PRO

Prepare the Peachy Summer Cheesecake on page 252, and serve it with ease. You'll need a sharp knife, some hot water and a towel. Dip the blade in water to heat, then wipe dry and cut. Repeat each time for pretty slices with a clean edge.

TEQUILA POACHED PEARS

Tequila may seem an unusual ingredient for a dessert, but give this one a try! The fresh pears and mint are so refreshing. Bring out this creative sweet when you want to impress guests.
—Nancy Heishman, Las Vegas, NV

Prep: 20 min. + simmering
Cook: 5 min.
Makes: 8 servings

- 2 cups water
- 1 can (11.3 oz.) pear nectar
- 1 cup tequila
- ½ cup sugar
- 2 Tbsp. lime juice
- 2 tsp. grated lime zest
- 1 cinnamon stick (3 in.)
- ¼ tsp. ground nutmeg
- 8 whole Anjou pears, peeled
  Sweetened whipped cream, optional
  Fresh mint leaves

1. Select saute setting on a 6-qt. pressure cooker and adjust for low heat. Add the first 8 ingredients; cook and stir until sugar is dissolved, about 3 minutes. Press cancel. Add pears. Lock lid; close pressure-release valve. Adjust to pressure-cook on high for 3 minutes. Quick-release pressure. Remove pears and keep warm. Press cancel.

2. Reserve 3 cups cooking juices; discard remaining juices and cinnamon stick. Return the reserved juices to pressure cooker. Select saute setting and adjust for medium heat. Simmer, uncovered, until liquid is reduced to 1 cup, about 30 minutes, stirring occasionally.

3. Halve pears lengthwise and core. Serve with the sauce, whipped cream if desired, and mint leaves.

1 PEAR WITH 2 TBSP. SAUCE: 155 cal., 0 fat (0 sat. fat), 0 chol., 3mg sod., 40g carb. (30g sugars, 6g fiber), 1g pro.

PUMPKIN FLANS

This silky, smooth dessert captures the essence and elegance of fall. I came up with the recipe myself, aiming to make something both luscious and light.
—Charles Insler, Silver Spring, MD

Prep: 45 min.
Cook: 15 min. + chilling
Makes: 6 servings

- 1 **cup sugar, divided**
- ¼ **cups water**
- 1½ **cups fat-free evaporated milk**
- 3 **large eggs**
- 1 **large egg white**
- ¼ **tsp. salt**
- ¼ **tsp. each ground ginger, cinnamon and cloves**
- 1 **cup canned pumpkin**
- 1 **tsp. vanilla extract**

TEST KITCHEN TIP
Flan is a sweet custard dessert that is often topped with a thin caramel sauce. Try making it with your own combination of spices and seasonings.

1. In a small heavy skillet over medium-low heat, combine ⅓ cup sugar and ¼ cup water. Cook, stirring occasionally, until sugar begins to melt. Cook without stirring until amber, about 20 minutes. Quickly pour into 6 ungreased 6-oz. ramekins or custard cups, tilting to coat bottoms of dishes. Let stand for 10 minutes.

2. In a small saucepan, heat milk until bubbles form around the sides of pan; remove from heat. In a large bowl, whisk eggs, egg white, salt, spices and remaining ⅔ cup sugar until blended but not foamy. Slowly stir in hot milk. Stir in pumpkin and vanilla. Slowly pour into prepared ramekins.

3. Cover each ramekin with foil. Place trivet insert and 1 cup water in pressure cooker. Set ramekins on trivet. Lock lid; close pressure-release valve. Adjust to pressure cook on high for 13 minutes. Quick-release pressure.

4. Centers should just be set (the mixture will jiggle) and a thermometer inserted in flan should read at least 160°. Carefully remove ramekins. Cool 10 minutes; refrigerate, covered, at least 4 hours. Carefully run a knife around the edges of ramekins to loosen; invert each dish onto a rimmed serving dish. If desired, sprinkle with additional cinnamon. Serve immediately.

1 SERVING: 235 cal., 3g fat (1g sat. fat), 96mg chol., 219mg sod., 45g carb. (42g sugars, 1g fiber), 9g pro.

LAVA CAKE

I love chocolate, and this decadent cake has long been a family favorite. It's even great cold the next day—assuming you have any leftovers!
—Elizabeth Farrell, Hamilton, MT

Prep: 15 min.
Cook: 20 min. + standing
Makes: 8 servings

- 1 cup all-purpose flour
- 1 cup packed brown sugar, divided
- 5 Tbsp. baking cocoa, divided
- 2 tsp. baking powder
- ¼ tsp. salt
- ½ cup fat-free milk
- 2 Tbsp. canola oil
- ½ tsp. vanilla extract
- ⅛ tsp. ground cinnamon
- 1¼ cups hot water
  Optional toppings:
    Fresh raspberries
    and ice cream

1. In a large bowl, whisk the flour, ½ cup brown sugar, 3 Tbsp. cocoa, baking powder and salt. In another bowl, whisk milk, oil and vanilla until blended. Add to flour mixture; stir just until moistened.

2. Spread into a 1½-qt. baking dish coated with cooking spray. In a small bowl, mix cinnamon and remaining ½ cup brown sugar and 2 Tbsp. cocoa; stir in hot water. Pour over batter (do not stir).

3. Place trivet insert and 1 cup water in a 6-qt. electric pressure cooker. Cover the baking dish with foil. Fold an 18x12-in. piece of foil lengthwise into thirds, making a sling. Use the sling to lower the dish onto the trivet. Lock lid; close pressure-release valve. Adjust to pressure-cook on high for 20 minutes. Quick-release pressure.

4. Using the foil sling, carefully remove baking dish. Let stand 15 minutes. A toothpick inserted in cake portion should come out clean.

1 SERVING: 208 cal., 4g fat (0 sat. fat), 0 chol., 208mg sod., 42g carb. (28g sugars, 1g fiber), 3g pro.

CRANBERRY STUFFED APPLES

Cinnamon, nutmeg and walnuts add to the homey flavor of these stuffed apples. What a lovely old-fashioned treat!
—Grace Sandvigen, Rochester, NY

Prep: 10 min.
Cook: 5 min.
Makes: 5 servings

- 5 **medium apples**
- ⅓ **cup fresh or frozen cranberries, thawed and chopped**
- ¼ **cup packed brown sugar**
- 2 **Tbsp. chopped walnuts**
- ¼ **tsp. ground cinnamon**
- ⅛ **tsp. ground nutmeg**
  Optional toppings:
  Whipped cream
  or vanilla ice cream

1. Core apples, leaving bottoms intact. Peel top third of each apple. Place trivet insert and 1 cup water in a 6-qt. electric pressure cooker. Combine the cranberries, brown sugar, walnuts, cinnamon and nutmeg; spoon into apples. Place apples on trivet.

2. Lock lid; close pressure-release valve. Adjust to pressure-cook on high for 3 minutes. Quick-release pressure. Serve with whipped cream or ice cream if desired.

1 STUFFED APPLE: 142 cal., 2g fat (0 sat. fat), 0 chol., 5mg sod., 33g carb. (27g sugars, 4g fiber), 1g pro. **DIABETIC EXCHANGES:** 1 starch, 1 fruit.

TEST KITCHEN TIP
The moisture in brown sugar tends to trap air between the crystals, so the sugar should be firmly packed when measuring, particularly when recipes specify "packed brown sugar" in the ingredient list.

PEACHY SUMMER CHEESECAKE

This is a cool, creamy, refreshing dessert that is special enough to take to a gathering. You can even prepare this ahead of time and freeze it. Just make sure you wrap it well so it's airtight, and add the peaches only after it thaws.
—Joan Engelhardt, Latrobe, PA

Prep: 25 min.
Cook: 30 min. + chilling
Makes: 6 servings

1 pkg. (8 oz.) reduced-fat cream cheese
4 oz. fat-free cream cheese
½ cup sugar
½ cup reduced-fat sour cream
2 Tbsp. unsweetened apple juice
1 Tbsp. all-purpose flour
½ tsp. vanilla
3 large eggs, room temperature, lightly beaten
2 medium ripe peaches, peeled and thinly sliced

1. Place the trivet insert and 1 cup water in a 6-qt. electric pressure cooker. Grease a 6-in. springform pan; place on a double thickness of heavy-duty foil (about 12 in. square). Wrap securely around pan.

2. In a large bowl, beat cream cheeses and sugar until smooth. Beat in sour cream, apple juice, flour and vanilla. Add eggs; beat on low speed just until blended. Pour into the prepared pan. Cover pan with foil. Fold an 18x12-in. piece of foil lengthwise into thirds, making a sling. Use the sling to lower the pan onto trivet.

3. Lock lid; close pressure-release valve. Adjust to pressure-cook on high for 30 minutes. Let pressure release naturally for 10 minutes; quick-release any remaining pressure. Using foil sling, carefully remove springform pan. Let stand 10 minutes. Remove foil from pan. Cool cheesecake on a wire rack 1 hour.

4. Loosen sides from pan with a knife. Refrigerate overnight, covering when cooled. To serve, remove rim from springform pan. Serve with peaches.

1 SLICE: 262 cal., 12g fat (7g sat. fat), 124mg chol., 342mg sod., 27g carb. (25g sugars, 1g fiber), 12g pro.

INDEX